ECCLESIASTES

STORIES TO LIVE BY

ECCLESIASTES
Stories to Live By

Translated, Edited and Compiled by

Joshua S. Sperka

BLOCH PUBLISHING CO.
New York

PREFACE

A new translation into modern idiom of the Book of Ecclesiastes, with an exciting story illustrating each verse, forms the uniqueness of this book.

This volume, the second publication in a series of the "Wisdom Literature" of the Bible, is in part an answer to contemporary needs. People seek guidance and purpose in the Book of books. However, the standard and revised translations of the Bible encounter a communication barrier. Language, usage, the denotation and connotation of words, change. Yet the modern reader is entitled to have the wisdom of the Bible available to him in a more accessible form. That is the reason for this new and original translation into clear, contemporary English.

The following verses are examples of the traditional translations compared with the translation as contained in this book.

(1:11) There is no remembrance of them of former times; neither shall there be any remembrance of them of latter times that are to come, among those that shall come after.

Former generations are not remembered. So, too, those who will come later will not be remembered by those who will succeed them.

(7:7) Surely oppression turneth a wise man into a fool; And a gift destroyeth the understanding.

For extortion deprives a wise man of reason, and a bribe corrupts the heart.

Another dramatic innovation of this work is that each verse is explained and illumined by a parable or a fable. In the classic tradition of amplifying Biblical passages, this book draws on the penetrating and succint wisdom of all ages, matching a story, fable or parable to each verse.

Ever since man began to express his ideas he sought a way to clarify abstract concepts. One literary form was the fable. These were stories in which imaginary animals speak and act like human beings and reflect human traits. Biblical commentators often employed fables to drive home a moral while entertaining their listeners.

A Talmudical story describes the function of the fable by the use, characteristically, of a parable. "Imagine a big basket full of produce without any handles, so that it could not be lifted. Then one clever man came and made handles for it and from that time on it was carried by the handles." (12:10, this book) The parable is the handle to the basket. It is easier to grasp penetrating truths and profound wisdom with the help of the parable.

The story simplifies the most intricate and abstract thoughts.

The story increases the ability of the reader to learn and to remember what he reads.

The story helps one to evaluate the failings of men as well as their virtues.

In this book you will find a rich and fascinating collection of parables, fables and stories covering a period of three thousand years. They range from earliest classical sources to those of the present day. Each verse is a self contained unit of reading matter.

The first volume in this project, *Proverbs to Live By*, was greeted in the New York Board of Rabbis Bulletin "as a welcome work most useful because of its topical arrangement and its appealingly refreshing translation." Jewish

Bookend of the Jewish Book Council of America praised the book in these words, "the author has earned our warm gratitude for the venturesome spirit that prompted this excellent work." This book has been transcribed into Braille for the blind and is now at the New York Institute for the Blind.

Many thanks to Rabbi Ephraim Sturm and to Mr. Nathan Saperstein of the National Council of Young Israel for their encouragement and the acceptance of my work as part of Young Israel's Institute for Jewish Studies.

I would like to acknowledge the cooperation given to me by my dear wife in typing, correcting and proofreading. My warm thanks to my scholarly son Shlomo for his help throughout the preparation of this book from the rough notes to the final manuscript.

—J. S. S.

TABLE OF CONTENTS

PREFACE

INTRODUCTION

The Book

What has made Ecclesiastes a book for all times is its depiction of man's search for meaning and purpose in life. What makes Ecclesiastes a book for our generation is that its author approaches the issues of life, its doubts and its questions, pragmatically as well as analytically.

This book is part of the "Wisdom Literature" of the Bible. The popular English title of the book is "Ecclesiastes." The title comes to us from the Septuagint, the Greek translation of the Bible and derives from the Hebrew "Koheleth," meaning assembly.

The Rabbis of the Talmud debated whether or not this book should become part of the Bible. It seemed to contain self-contradictions and thoughts of pessimism and epicurianism that might mislead the reader. But since the book ultimately taught the observance of divine precepts and fear of God it was included in the Bible.

Tradition ascribes the authorship of the book to King Solomon, and its final editing to the wise men of the Court of King Hezekiah (562-531 B.C.E.). In the past century Biblical scholars of the school of higher criticism have made a sport of belittling the traditional authorship of the Bible. Theories of dates, composition and authorship of the book changed as often as women's fashions. Modern scholars saw in the book the product or reflections of Greek philosophy, secularism, agnosticism and hedonism.

13

One scholar advanced the theory that this little book, consisting of only twelve chapters, was not written by Solomon but by nine different authors. Another writer suggested that this book, consisting of 222 verses, had 120 interpolators. It is not surprising that we find in a more recent book, *Koheleth, Man and His World,* by Dr. Robert Gordis, the statements that "A few decades ago when the theory was widely held that Koheleth was a disciple of Greek philosophy, linguistic parallels from Greek were often proposed. Close study of both the substance and the form of the book has made it clear that there is no indubitable Greek construction or idioms in the text, and not a single instance of a Greek word," and "The various Hakam glossators and Hasid interpolators are merely figments of the scholarly imagination." (p. 62)

The Message

The book opens with the pessimistic premise: "Vanity of vanities, all is vanity," that man has no earthly gain "from all his labor under the sun."

The author begins to experiment with, and test, accepted values of life. He reappraises wisdom. He tests pleasure and the amassing of wealth. He discovers that wisdom increases pain, that pleasure is ephemeral and passing, and that hard earned wealth inevitably is left to someone else, who has not labored for it. He then turns from the personal to the collective experience. He looks for justice among men, but "in the place of justice there is iniquity." The powerful and the "officials oppress the weak and the poor." He sees the just suffer and the unjust prosper. The end of man is death. It seems that the wise, the fool and even the animals all meet a common end. All this leads him to a sceptical attitude and a feeling of futility. If life is so bad, why go on living?

Koheleth is unique in that in spite of this pessimistic question the book is not pervaded with a sense of gloom and tragedy. The book suggests an answer to this basic question. There is something positive and affirmative in life. Man has the ability and the duty to face up to the problems of life. In his search for purpose man will find the purpose of his search. In this search, he will find satisfaction. The wise man and the fool die, but still "wisdom excels folly as light excels darkness." It is true that the rich, the miser and the poor all meet the same end, but he who enjoys his possessions has received a gift from God. Even striving for happiness can become a reasonable goal.

This book expresses scepticism, pessimism and determinism, as well as faith. These are the changing moods and the successive views of a thinking man rather than simply disconnected ruminations. The underlying unity of thought and belief in the book despite apparently startling contradictions, is illustrated in this story.

The sun and the moon met. The moon complained about its unfortunate lot in the world. "You the sun, you shine, you bring warmth and light to man. I shine in the night time and even during the freezing winter nights." The sun reacted with sympathy and said, "Since you must serve in the severe, frosty nights let us order a cloak for you for the winter season." All the tailors in the world were summoned to fashion a cloak for the moon. None would accept the order. "How can we make a coat for one whose shape and size is constantly changing. Sometimes the moon is small and thin, then it grows to half a circle, then it develops into a round, fat, full circle."

Man too, does not remain static. His thoughts and opinions change with his experience and knowledge. What a modern writer once said about another book applies to this one: "Comrade, this is no book. Who touches this touches a man."

Koheleth teaches his basic principles directly and indirectly. The existence of the world proves the existence of God. God created man as he created man's instincts and his limitations. "Man cannot comprehend the meaning of that which happens under the sun. No matter how much a man will labor to seek it he will not fathom it; and even if a wise man should determine to know, he will not be able to grasp it." (8:17) This does not deny divine rule or detract from the divine dignity of the universe. One must not confuse hidden purpose with no purpose. This incomprehensibility is due to man's earthly restrictions and his intellectual limitations and does not indicate the absence of an underlying divine plan. Man cannot find the purpose of life, but not because there is no meaning to it. Just as there is design in nature there is purpose in the destiny of man, but man is unable to grasp it. This, then, is the final appeal of the book, "Fear God and keep the commandment."

ECCLESIASTES

STORIES TO LIVE BY

ECCLESIASTES

CHAPTER ONE

1. The words of Koheleth, the son of David, King in Jerusalem.

2. "Vanity of vanities," says Koheleth, "Vanity of vanities, all is vanity."

3. What does a man gain from all his labor that he toils under the sun?

4. A generation goes and a generation comes while the earth endures forever.

5. The sun rises and the sun sets and hastens to the place where it is to rise.

6. Blowing towards the south and circling to the north, the wind goes round and round and returns on its course.

7. All rivers flow into the sea yet the sea is never full; to the place where the rivers flow, there they continue to flow.

8. All things are wearisome, no man is able to describe it; the eye is never satisfied with seeing nor the ear filled with hearing.

9. What has been that will be, and what has happened that will happen; and there is nothing new under the sun.

10. There is something about which one may say, "Look this is new"; it existed long ago, before our time.

11. Former generations are not remembered. So, too, those who will come later will not be remembered by those who will succeed them.

12. I, Koheleth, was King of Israel in Jerusalem.

13. I directed my heart to search and to explore with wisdom everything that happens beneath the heavens. It is a sorry task that God has given men with which to occupy themselves.

14. I observed everything that happens under the sun and it seems that all is futile and a striving after wind.

15. What is crooked cannot be made straight, what is missing cannot be counted.

16. I said to myself, "Indeed, I have become great and acquired wisdom above all who preceded me in Jerusalem, and my heart has perceived much wisdom and knowledge."

17. I directed my heart to knowing wisdom and to knowing madness and folly. I am convinced that this, too, is striving after wind.

18. For the more wisdom the more grief; and he who increases knowledge increases pain.

CHAPTER TWO

1. I said to myself, "Come now, I will test you with pleasure and have a good time." But this too turned out to be futile.

2. Of merrymaking I concluded, "It is folly" and of pleasure, "What does it accomplish?"

3. I resolved in my heart to indulge my body with wine while my mind was acting with wisdom and grasping folly, until I might discover what course is best for men to follow in their brief span of life under heaven.

4. I extended my enterprises, I built mansions for myself and I planted vineyards for myself.

5. I laid out gardens and orchards and I planted in them all kinds of fruit trees.

6. I constructed pools of water to irrigate the forest of sprouting trees.

7. I acquired male and female slaves and I had house-

born servants. I also owned much cattle and sheep, more than anyone who preceded me in Jerusalem.

8. I collected for myself silver and gold and the treasures of kings and provinces. I obtained for myself male and female singers, man's delights, coaches and chariots.

9. So I became great and surpassed all my predecessors in Jerusalem. Indeed, my wisdom stood by me.

10. I did not withhold anything that my eyes desired, I did not deny myself any pleasure for my heart rejoiced in all my labor; and this was my reward for all my effort.

11. Then I examined all the accomplishments that my hands had built up and the possessions that I toiled to acquire, and all seemed futile and striving after wind. And there is no gain under the sun.

12. I then turned to observe wisdom, hilarity and folly; for what can the man do who comes after the king? That which he has already done!

13. Then I perceived that wisdom excels folly as light excels darkness.

14. The wise man has his eyes in his head but the fool walks in darkness; but I also realized that the same fate overtakes them all.

15. Then I reflected in my heart. Since what may happen to the fool will also happen to me, of what use was it then for me to have become so extremely wise? And I concluded that this, too, is futility.

16. For the wise man is no more remembered forever than the fool; in the days to come all will be forgotten. How the wise man dies just like the fool!

17. So I was disgusted with life. For I was depressed by all that goes on under the sun, because all seems futile and a striving after wind.

18. And I detested all my wealth which I had achieved under the sun, for I must leave it to the man who will succeed me.

19. And who knows whether he will be a wise man or a fool? Yet he will control all my possessions for which I

21

exerted toil and exercised wisdom under the sun; this, also, is futility.

20. I turned to view with despair all the gains for which I toiled under the sun.

21. For here is a man who has labored with wisdom, intelligence and success and yet must leave his property to a man who has not toiled for it. This, too, is futility and a great misfortune.

22. For what has a man of all his labor and of the striving of his heart for which he toils under the sun?

23. For all his days are painful and his business provoking and even at night his mind has no rest. This, too, is vanity.

24. There is nothing better for man but that he eat and drink and find satisfaction in his work. This, also, I perceived is a gift of God.

25. For who should eat and who enjoy, except I?

26. He grants wisdom, knowledge and happiness to the person who pleases Him, but to the sinner He assigns the task of gathering and amassing so that he may leave it to one who is pleasing to God. This, also, is vanity and striving after wind.

CHAPTER THREE

1. For everything there is a season and a time for every experience under heaven.

2. A time to be born and a time to die; a time to plant and a time to uproot what is planted.

3. A time to kill and a time to heal; a time to break down and a time to build up.

4. A time to cry and a time to laugh; a time to mourn and a time to dance.

5. A time to scatter stones and a time to gather stones; a time to embrace and a time to refrain from embracing.

6. A time to seek and a time to lose; a time to guard and a time to discard.

7. A time to rend and a time to mend; a time to be silent and a time to speak.

8. A time to love and a time to hate; a time for war and a time for peace.

9. What does the worker gain by his effort?

10. I have considered the task which God has given to men to occupy themselves with.

11. He has made everything properly in its time; He also put eternity in their hearts, but man can never comprehend the plan of God's work in its entirety.

12. I realized that there is nothing better for them than to be happy and to do good in their lifetime.

13. Indeed any man who eats and drinks and finds satisfaction in his occupation, that is a gift of God.

14. I realized that whatever God ordains shall be forever; nothing can be added to it, and from it nothing can be subtracted. God has done this that man may revere Him.

15. Whatever is has been long ago and what is to be has been long ago; God will seek the pursued.

16. Furthermore, I observed under the sun that in the place of justice there was iniquity and in the place of equity there was wickedness.

17. I reflected in my heart, "God will judge the innocent and the guilty, for there is a time for every experience and every act—there."

18. I reflected with regard to men that God might make it clear to them so that they may see that by themselves they are but beasts.

19. For that which happens to man happens to the beast; the same fate befalls them; as one dies, so does the other; the same breath is in all of them; and man has no advantage over the beast, for all is vanity.

20. All go to one place, all are from dust and all return to dust.

21. Who knows the spirit of man that ascends upward and the spirit of the beast that descends downward to the earth.

22. So it appeared to me that there is nothing better for man than to be happy in his activities for that is his lot, for who can cause him to see what will be after him.

CHAPTER FOUR

1. I reconsidered all the oppressions practiced under the sun; and there were the tears of the oppressed and they had none to comfort them. In the hands of their oppressors was power, but they had none to comfort them.

2. I regarded as more fortunate the dead who have already died, than the living who are still alive.

3. But better off than either is the one who has never been, who has never seen the evil deeds done under the sun.

4. I have observed that all effort and skill in work spring from man's rivalry with his neighbor. This, too, is vanity and a striving after wind.

5. The fool folds his hands and he devours his own flesh.

6. Better a handful with ease than two handfuls with toil and striving after wind.

7. Again I observed an absurdity under the sun.

8. There is a lone man, with no companion, who has neither son nor brother; but there is no end to all his toil, nor is his eye ever satisfied with riches. "For whom am I toiling and depriving myself of pleasure?" This, too, is futility and a miserable task.

9. Two are better than one, because they have a better reward for their labor.

10. For if they fall one will lift up his companion, but woe to him who is alone and falls with no one to lift him.

11. Also, if two huddle together they keep warm, but how can one alone be warm?

12. If one should attack, two can stand up against him and "a threefold cord is not easily broken."

13. Better a poor but wise youth, than an old but foolish king who no longer knows to heed a warning.

14. For one may come out of prison to govern, while the other even in his royalty becomes poor.

15. I have seen all the people who walk under the sun with the youthful successor who was to replace him (the king).

16. There was no end to all the people, to all whose leader he was; nevertheless, later generations will not be happy with him. Surely, this, too, is vanity and a striving after wind.

17. Guard your steps when you go to the House of God. More acceptable is obedience than the offering of a sacrifice by fools; for they do not realize that they do wrong.

CHAPTER FIVE

1. Never be rash with your speech; never let your heart be hasty to express words before God; for God is in Heaven and you are on earth; therefore let your words be few.

2. As a dream comes because of many concerns, so the fool speaks in many words.

3. When you make a vow to God do not delay fulfilling it, for He has no pleasure in fools. Whatever you vow, fulfill.

4. It is better not to vow, than to vow and not fulfill.

5. Let not your mouth cause guilt to your body and plead not before the messenger, "It was a mistake." Why should God be angry at your speech and destroy what you have accomplished.

6. Multitudes of dreams and vanities result in a multitude of words; but you fear God.

7. If you see the exploitation of the poor and the perversion of justice and righteousness in the state, do not be perplexed at the situation, for there is an official watching an official and over them are higher officials.

8. The advantage of land is above all else, even the king is devoted to the soil.

9. He who loves money is never satisfied with money

and he who loves riches never has enough income; this, too, is vanity.

10. When prosperity increases, they increase who consume it; then of what value is it to its owner except feasting his eyes.

11. Sweet is the sleep of the laborer whether he eat little or much, but the over-abundance of the rich man will not let him sleep.

12. There is a painful evil which I have seen under the sun: wealth hoarded by its owner to his own hurt.

13. His wealth is lost through a bad investment and then a son is born to him and he has nothing left in his hand.

14. As he came from his mother's womb, naked shall he return, going as he came; and for his toil he has nothing to take with him.

15. And this, too, is a painful evil, exactly as he came he must depart; so what profit has he who toils for the wind?

16. All his days he even eats in the dark and he has much grief, illness and anger.

17. Behold, this is what I have observed: it is good and proper to eat and drink and to enjoy pleasure with all the gains one has earned under the sun during the span of life which God has allotted to one, for that is one's lot.

18. Furthermore, every man to whom God has given wealth, possessions and the power to enjoy it, to take his portion and be happy in his work, this is a gift of God.

19. For let him remember that the days of his life are not many; that God has decreed the joy of his heart.

CHAPTER SIX

1. There is an evil which I observed under the sun and it is prevalent among men.

2. A man to whom God grants wealth, possessions and position so that he lacks nothing he may desire, but God has not given him power to enjoy it, for some stranger will consume it. This is vanity and an evil affliction.

3. If a man has a hundred children and lives many years, be his life ever so long, but he derives no satisfaction from his wealth, were he to have no burial, I declare that a stillborn child is better off than he.

4. For it (the stillborn) comes in vain and departs in darkness and its name will be shrouded in darkness;

5. It has neither seen nor known the sun. This has more rest than the other.

6. Even if one lives twice a thousand years and experiences no contentment, do not all go to the same place?

7. All a man's toil is for his mouth, and yet his appetite is never satisfied.

8. For what advantage has a wise man over a fool or a poor man who knows how to face the problems of life?

9. Better is what the eyes can see than the pursuit of desire, this, too, is vanity and a striving after wind.

10. Whatever happens has been ordained long ago and it is known what man is, that he cannot contend with what is mightier than he.

11. Since many possessions increase vanity, of what advantage are they to man?

12. Who knows what is good for man in his life, the numbered days of his futile existence, which pass like a shadow? Who can tell a man what will happen after him under the sun?

CHAPTER SEVEN

1. A good name is better than good oil and the day of death than the day of one's birth.

2. It is better to go to the house of mourning than to go to the house of feasting because that is the end of every man, and the living will take it to heart.

3. Seriousness is better than laughter, for through sadness of face the heart improves.

4. The heart of the wise is in the house of mourning, but the heart of fools is in the house of amusement.

5. It is better to listen to the censure of the wise than for one to listen to the praise of fools.

6. Like the noise of thorns under a pot, so is the laughter of the fool; this, too, is vanity.

7. For extortion deprives a wise man of reason and a bribe corrupts the heart.

8. Better is the end of a matter than its beginning. Better is patience than pride.

9. Do not quickly give way to anger, for anger rests in the bosom of fools.

10. Do not say, "How is it that the former days were better than these?" It is not out of wisdom that you have asked about this.

11. Wisdom with inheritance is good and an advantage to those who see the sun.

12. For wisdom is a shelter as money is a shelter, and the advantage of knowledge is that wisdom preserves the life of those who possess it.

13. Consider the work of God, for who can straighten what He has made bent.

14. In the day of good fortune enjoy yourself and in the day of misfortune consider; God has ordained one to balance the other, to the end that man is unable to foresee his future.

15. I have seen all things in my fleeting days, sometimes a just man perishes in spite of his justice and sometimes a wicked man endures in spite of his wickedness.

16. Be not excessively righteous nor excessively wise, why should you be forsaken?

17. Be not excessively wicked nor be a fool, why should you die before your time?

18. It is well to grasp one and also do not let go of the other; for he who fears God will consider both.

19. Wisdom gives a wise man strength, more than ten rulers that were in a city.

20. For no man on earth is righteous who always does good and never sins.

21. Furthermore, pay no attention to every word that is spoken lest you hear your servant insult you.

22. For you know in your heart that many times you yourself have insulted others.

23. All this I tested with wisdom. I said, "I will be wise," but it was unattainable.

24. Inconceivable is that which exists and very mystifying, who can fathom it?

25. I determined in my heart to study, to search and to seek wisdom and meaning; to learn that wickedness is folly and stupidity is madness.

26. And I find more bitter than death the woman whose heart is snares and nets, her hands chains. He who is pleasing to God will escape her but the sinner will be trapped by her.

27. Behold, this I have found, says Koheleth, adding one to one to reach a solution.

28. What I am still looking for but did not find; one man out of a thousand I found, but one woman among all these I have not found.

29. Behold, this only have I discovered, that God made men upright but they have sought many devices.

CHAPTER EIGHT

1. Who can compare with the wise man? And who knows the interpretation of an event? A man's wisdom illumines his face and the harshness of his features is changed.

2. I obey the king's command because of the oath taken before God.

3. Do not hurry to leave his presence; do not persist in a bad cause, for he does whatever he pleases.

4. Inasmuch as the word of the king is supreme; and who can say to him, "What are you doing?"

5. He who obeys the commandments will experience no harm; and a wise heart senses the time and judgment.

6. For every matter has its time and judgment, for the tyranny of man is heavy upon him.

7. For no one knows what shall be, for who can tell him when it shall be?

8. No man has power over his spirit to restrain the spirit, neither has he control over the day of death; no substitute can be sent into battle, neither will evil schemes rescue its owners.

9. All this I have seen, and I have applied my heart to everything that happened under the sun, at a time when man has power to harm his fellow man.

10. And so I have seen wicked men buried and they came to rest, and those who did right depart from the place of the holy and were forgotten in the city. This, too, is vanity.

11. Because the sentence against crime is not promptly executed, that is why man's heart is inclined to do evil.

12. Even though the sinner does wrong a hundred times and his punishment is delayed, nevertheless I know it will be well with the God fearing who revere God.

13. And it shall not be well with the wicked, but like a shadow, he shall not prolong his days because he does not fear God.

14. There is an illusion that exists on earth; sometimes just men are treated according to the conduct of the wicked and sometimes wicked men are treated according to the conduct of the just. I said that this, too, is an illusion.

15. And I praised enjoyment because a man has nothing better under the sun than to eat and to drink and be happy and have this accompany him in his toil, during the span of his life allotted to him by God under the sun.

16. I set my heart to study wisdom and to consider the activity which takes place on earth; even to deprive oneself of sleep day and night.

17. I realized that it is all the work of God. Man cannot comprehend the meaning of that which happens under the sun. No matter how much a man will labor to seek it, he

will not fathom it; and even if a wise man should determine to know he will not be able to grasp it.

CHAPTER NINE

1. For all this I took to heart to clarify all this, that the just and the wise and their actions are in God's hands; man does not know whether he will be in favor or disfavor. All is ordained before them.

2. The same fate awaits all. One event to the just and the unjust; to the good and to the clean and to the unclean; to the one who sacrifices and the one who does not sacrifice. As is the good, so is the sinner; he who takes an oath, as he who fears an oath.

3. This is an evil in all that is done under the sun, that there is one fate for all. Therefore the heart of man is full of evil, and madness is in their minds while they live and after that they join the dead.

4. For he who is classed among the living has hope, for a live dog is better than a dead lion.

5. For the living know that they will die but the dead know nothing; they no longer receive reward. Even their memory is forgotten.

6. Their loves, their hates and their jealousies have already perished; they have no further share forever in all that happens under the sun.

7. Go, eat your bread with joy and drink your wine with a happy heart, for God has already approved your actions.

8. Let your garments always be white and your head never lack ointment.

9. Enjoy life with the woman you love, all the fleeting days of your life which He has given you under the sun, throughout your brief days, for that is your share in life and for all the effort of your toil under the sun.

10. Whatever you are able to achieve do while you have strength, for there is no action nor plan, no knowledge nor wisdom in the grave where you are going.

11. Again I observed under the sun that the race is not to the swift nor the battle to the brave, nor is there bread for the wise, nor riches for the intelligent, nor favor for scholars, for all are victims of time and chance.

12. Furthermore, man never knows his time; like fish caught in an evil net, as birds trapped in a snare, so men are trapped in an hour of calamity as it falls upon them suddenly.

13. This also I saw as a bit of wisdom under the sun and it greatly impressed me.

14. There was a small city with few men in it and a powerful king came and surrounded it and built great siege works over it.

15. Now, there was found in it a poor, wise man, who by his wisdom rescued the city. Yet no one remembered that poor man.

16. So I reflected, wisdom is better than strength, yet the poor man's wisdom is despised and his words are not accepted.

17. The words of the wise spoken softly are more acceptable than the shouting of the king of fools.

18. Wisdom is better than weapons of war but one sinner destroys much good.

CHAPTER TEN

1. As dead flies befoul and corrupt the perfumer's ointment, so a little folly can outweigh wisdom and honor.

2. A wise man's heart keeps him to the right and a fool's to the left.

3. As the fool walks on the road he lacks proper sense and proclaims to all that he is a fool.

4. If the temper of the ruler is aroused against you, do not resign your post, for mildness appeases great offenses.

5. There is an evil which I observed under the sun that is like an error committed by a despot.

6. Folly is placed in high positions while the noble sit in low places.

7. I have seen slaves upon horses while princes were walking on the ground like slaves.

8. He who digs a pit will fall into it and he who breaks down a fence will be bitten by a snake.

9. He who removes stones may be hurt by them; he who splits logs may be harmed by them.

10. If an ax is dull and one does not sharpen its edge, one must exert more strength. There is an advantage in wise preparation.

11. If a serpent bites before being charmed what is the use of having a trained charmer?

12. Words from the mouth of a wise man gain favor but the lips of a fool destroy him.

13. The beginning of his speech is foolishness and the end of his speech is mischievous madness.

14. A fool multiplies words. Man does not know what is about to be, who can tell him what will happen after that.

15. The efforts of the fool exhaust him so that he does not know his way to the city.

16. Woe to you, O land, when your king is a youth and your princes feast in the morning.

17. Happy are you, O land, when your king is a free man and your princes feast at the proper time, with restraint and not in drunkenness.

18. Through idleness the roof sinks and through laziness the house becomes flooded.

19. A feast is made for levity and wine to cheer life, and money answers it all.

20. Do not curse the king even in your thoughts, nor curse a rich man in your chamber, for a bird in the air may carry the report, and a winged creature relate the matter.

CHAPTER ELEVEN

1. Cast your bread upon the waters for after many days you will find it.

2. Give a portion to seven and even to eight, for you never know what misfortune will happen in the land.

3. If the clouds be filled with rain they empty out on the earth; if a tree falls southward or northward, where the tree falls there it will remain.

4. A wind watcher will never sow, and a cloud gazer will never reap.

5. As you do not know the course of the wind nor what is the embryo in a pregnant womb, so you cannot know the actions of God who has created all.

6. In the morning sow your seed and in the evening let not your hand rest for you never know which will excel, one or the other, or if both may turn out equally well.

7. Sweet is the light and pleasant for the eyes to see the sunshine.

8. Though a man live many years let him be happy in all of them and let him remember that the days of darkness will be many; all that is coming is futility.

9. Be happy, young man, in your youth and let your heart cheer you in the days of your manhood; follow the inclinations of your heart and the sight of your eyes; but know that for all this God will bring you to account.

10. Banish anger from your heart and avoid abuse of your body; for youth and manhood are fleeting.

CHAPTER TWELVE

1. Remember your Creator in the days of your vigor before the days of trouble come and the years are reached when you will say, "I have no pleasure in them."

2. Before the sun and the light and the moon and the stars grow dark and the clouds return after the rain.

3. In the day when the guards of the house become shaky and the strong men will stoop, and the grinders cease

because they are few and those that look out the windows are dimmed.

4. The doors to the street are shut, as the sound of the mill is low and one wakes at the song of a bird and all the strains of music are hushed.

5. They are afraid of every height and of the terrors on the road; and the almond tree blossoms and the grasshopper is a burden and the caperberry is impotent; because man goes to his eternal home and the mourners go about in the street.

6. Before the silver cord is parted and the golden bowl is shattered and the pitcher is broken at the fountain and the wheel is smashed into the well.

7. And the dust returns to the earth as it was and the spirit returns to God who gave it.

8. Vanity of vanities, says Koheleth, all is illusion.

9. In addition to Koheleth having been a wise man he also taught the people knowledge. Pondering and searching, he composed many parables.

10. Koheleth tried to find acceptable subjects and that which is properly written, words of truth.

11. The words of the wise are like goads and like well fastened nails are the words of the masters of assemblies. They were given by one Shepherd.

12. Of more than these be warned, my son, of making many books there is no end and excessive studying is physically exhausting.

13. The sum of the matter, all having been heard; fear God and keep His commandments for this is the whole duty of man.

14. For every deed whether good or bad, even those hidden, God will bring into judgment.

CHAPTER ONE

1. *The Words of Koheleth, the son of David, King in Jerusalem.*

The Book of Ecclesiastes is enriched through three unique strengths of the author. He possessed personal perception, he had learned the wisdom of the past, and had reaped the experience of a king. These three sources of understanding are indicated in the opening sentence. The phrase "The Words of Koheleth" indicates that his words were accepted in "Kahal," the assembly because he personified wisdom. "The son of David," he is the son of a king with a royal background which linked him to the wisdom of the past. "King in Jerusalem," the city famed for wisdom provided an opportunity to explore and experiment with the philosophy he taught.

He (Solomon) wrote three books: Song of Songs, Proverbs and this book, Ecclesiastes. Which one was written first? Rabbi Cheyah said he wrote Proverbs first, then Song of Songs and then Ecclesiastes. Rabbi Jonathan said he wrote Song of Songs first, then Proverbs and then Ecclesiastes. Rabbi Jonathan based this on a man's way in the world. When a man is young he composes songs; when he matures he writes proverbial maxims; when he becomes old he writes about the vanity of things.

—Midrash Rabbah, Song of Songs I

2. *"Vanity of vanities," says Koheleth, "Vanity of vanities, all is vanity."*

The word "vanity" in this verse occurs twice in plural form, which equals four, and three times in the singular for a total of seven. The midrash sees in these seven repetitions a reference to the seven stages of a man's life emphasizing that all of life is vanity.

"The Seven Vanities" mentioned by Koheleth correspond to the seven stages which a man goes through in his lifetime. At the age of one year he is like a king; everyone embraces and kisses him. At the age of two and three he is like a pig playing with dirt in the gutters. At the age of ten he skips like a goat. At the age of twenty he is like a neighing horse adorning himself and yearning for a wife. He marries and assumes burdens like a donkey. When he has children he becomes aggressive as a dog to provide their food and needs. When he becomes old he is bent like an ape.

—Midrash Rabbah, Ecclesiastes I

3. *What does a man gain from all his labor that he toils under the sun?*

What does a man gain.

It happened that a fox had been without food for a long time. After weeks of searching he noticed a fruit orchard in the distance. Happily he approached the orchard seeking an entrance but he could find no gate nor entrance. Round and round he circled the fence, but saw no door. He finally found a small opening in the fence but it was too small for him to go through.

At the end of the day he resolved to fast and reduce his size so that he could enter through this small opening. He succeeded in his plan and finally entered the vineyard. Never in his life had he enjoyed so much and such excellent food. He grew fat so that when he wished to go out, he could not leave.

Again he fasted and starved himself in order to be able to leave through the same small opening through which he had entered. Following this painful process, the fox, now on the outside, looked back at the vineyard and said, "How good and pleasant is your fruit, but what did I gain. I had to leave as I came in." Such is this world.

—Midrash Rabbah, Ecclesiastes V

4. *A generation goes and a generation comes while the earth endures forever.*

The author contrasts the transitory character of life with the abiding setting of the earth, as each generation passes on to make room for the next.

There was once a king who ruled his kingdom with fairness and justice. He had established a great empire and conquered many lands. He had won the respect and loyalty of all his subjects. What troubled him was that some day when he will become old and die he would have to leave it all.

One day the king said to one of his wise counsellors, the philosopher of his realm, "Sweet would be a king's lot if it lasted forever."

The wise man replied, "Had such been your predecessor's fate, how would you have reached the throne?" "My Lord," the wise man continued, "I also thought that there is something unfair in the universe when death destroys growth in nature and in man. The problem gave me no rest. Day and night I searched for an answer to this question. One night I dreamed that my quest was granted. I found myself living in a world where neither nature nor man knew death. All human beings lived on. No man died. No flower faded. No tree lost its foilage. In time I realized that this was an undesirable change. Nothing died, but nothing was born. When death was eliminated, birth was eliminated."

—Oral Tradition

5. *The sun rises and the sun sets and hastens to the place where it is to rise.*

To us sunrise and sunset are familiar phenomenon. To Adam, the first man, the first sunset was novel and perplexing.

When Adam on the day of his creation and after disobeying God's command saw the setting of the sun he cried out: "It is because I have sinned that the world about me is becoming dark. The universe will return to chaos and confusion. This then is the death to which I have been sentenced from Heaven."

He sat awake all night fasting and weeping. Eve also was crying opposite him. However, when dawn appeared Adam said, "This is the usual course of the world."

We are further told: When Adam, the first man, saw that each day was becoming shorter (the sun set earlier) he said, "Perhaps this is happening because I have sinned. The world is being darkened and the universe will become again void and without form. This then is the kind of death decreed upon me from Heaven." He began keeping an eight day fast. But as he observed the winter equinox after the month of Teveth and saw that the days were getting longer, he said, "Such is the order of the world."

—Talmud, Avoda Zora p. 8a

6. *Blowing towards the south and circling to the north, the wind goes round and round and returns on its course.*

Blowing towards the south and circling to the north.

In this and the preceding and succeeding sentences the author speaks of the sun, the wind and water as three elements of nature who do their repetitious tasks day after day. In a work of the second century a similar thought is found. "When the Lord created His works in the beginning, He fixed the various divisions after He made them. He established His works in a system forever and their missions for all generations. They do not grow hungry or tired and they do not cease to function. None of them crowds his neighbors and they never disobey His command."

—Wisdom of Ben Sira 17:26-28

7. *All rivers flow into the sea yet the sea is never full; to the place where the rivers flow, there they continue to flow.*

This prosaic description of the waters following a static law of nature is imbued by the Rabbis of the Midrash with life, as well as with an ethical admonition.

Following the creation of the world the waters rose until they almost reached the throne of Glory. Then the Almighty cried out, "Be still, O waters." Then the waters became vainglorious and boasted, "We are the mightiest of all creation, let us flood the earth!" At this, God grew angry and rebuked the waters, "Do not boast of your strength, you vain braggarts. I will send a barrier of sand against you!" When the waters saw the sand consisting of tiny grains they mocked, "How can such tiny grains stand up against us? One little wave will sweep them away." When the grains of sand heard this they grew frightened. But their leader comforted them and said: "Do not be afraid. True, we are tiny and each alone is insignificant, but if we remain united the waters will see what power we have." When the tiny grains of sand heard these words of comfort they came flying from all the corners of the earth and lay down one on top of the other upon the shores of the seas. They rose up and formed a huge barrier against the waters. And when the waters saw

how the great army of the grains of sand stood united they
became frightened and retreated.

—Midrash, Tehillim 93

8. *All things are wearisome, no man is able to describe
it; the eye is never satisfied with seeing nor the ear filled
with hearing.*

King Alexander of Macedonia, world conqueror of
ancient times, is taught in this legend the meaning of the
"eye is never satisfied with seeing."

"Open up the Gates," he cried out. "King Alexander wants
to enter." Instantly the answer came, "These are the gates
of the Eternal. Only the pious may enter here." Seeing the
Gates would not open he pleaded, "Give me some kind of
token, O Heavenly Gates, so that I can prove that I've been
here." At this the Gates of Paradise opened for an instant.
A human eye rolled toward him. Amazed, Alexander picked
it up and placed it in his knapsack. Then he traveled back
to Macedonia.

No sooner had he reached home than he called his wise
men together. He told them everything that had happened
to him. "What signifies the strange gift I received?" he
asked. "O King," replied the wise men, "place the eye in the
scales and weigh it." "What for?" asked Alexander, "I can
tell you beforehand that it weighs but little." "Please do
place it," the wise men urged. "In the other half of the
scales place a gold piece. Then we will find out which is
heavier."

Alexander did as they asked. To his surprise he found
that the eye was heavier than the gold piece. He threw into
the scales another gold coin, still the eye was heavier. He
then threw in a whole handful of coins and ordered that all
his gold and silver and jewels be thrown in. Still the eye
outweighed the treasure. "Even were you to take all your
chariots and horses and palaces and place them in the scale,

the eye will still be heavier," said the wise men. "How do you explain this?" asked the king. "How is such a thing possible?" "Learn a lesson from this," said the wise men. "Know that the human eye is never satisfied with what it sees. No matter how much treasure you will show it, it will want more and still more." "Your explanation does not satisfy me, give me proof," insisted Alexander. "Very well," agreed the wise men. "Have all your gold and treasure removed from the scales. Then place a pinch of dust in their place and observe what happens."

Barely had Alexander placed a little dust in the scales when they tipped to the other end, for the dust proved heavier than the eye. "Now I understand the meaning of your words and what was in your minds," said the King. "So long as man is alive, his eye is never satisfied. No sooner does he die then he is dust. Then the eye loses desire."

—Talmud, Tammid p. 32b

9. *What has been that will be and what has happened that will happen; and there is nothing new under the sun.*

The author ventures to declare that the discoveries of his day are not "new."

Fifteen hundred years before Copernicus (1473-1543) who is credited with discovering that the earth and other planets revolve around the sun, the Rabbis of the Talmud declared that the earth is like a globe (not flat). All the planets revolve around the sun like a ball, some are over and some are below.

—Zohar, Vayikra 3:1
Jerusalem Talmud, Avoda Zora 3:1
Midrash Rabbah, Bamidbar:Nasso:13

Astronomers of old spoke of several thousand stars. In the Talmud Brochoth (p. 32) the estimate of stars runs into the tens of millions. The planets are in constant motion.

43

Rabbi Nachman said, "The sultry air of the sun produced by the passage of the sun's rays (ultra violet) through a cloudy atmosphere is more intense than that of direct sunlight.

—Talmud, Yoma p. 28b

10. *There is something about which one may say, "Look, this is new;" it existed long ago before our time.*

Continuing the theme of the previous verse the thought stated in this sentence is that many "new" discoveries were known "long before our time."

Rabbi Gamliel had a tube (telescope) through which he could see objects at a distance of 2000 cubits across the land and a corresponding distance across the sea. Anyone who wanted to know the exact depth of a valley could discover it with a tube. Anyone who wanted to know the height of a palm tree looked through the tube and measured the shadows compared with the shadow cast by a man whose height was known.

—Talmud, Eruvin p. 43b

In the year 1720, long before Alexander Graham Bell, a question was asked: Is it permitted on the Sabbath to speak into an instrument capable of transmitting the human voice over distant miles?

—David Oppenheimer, Tshuvos Yaakov
Prague 5482-1720

Benjamin Franklin (1706-1790) discovered that lightning is an electrical discharge. In Talmudical writings 1500 years earlier this law was discussed: "If one places an iron bar among fowl to ward off bad luck, it is forbidden as superstition; but if it is done because of electrical storms or at a time of lightning, it is permitted."

—Tosefta, Sabbath Chapter 7:10

11. *Former generations are not remembered. So, too, those who will come later will not be remembered by those who will succeed them.*

To support his assertion of the vanity of life the author proclaims the sad fact that even fame does not last forever as illustrated by the sequence from Joseph's experience in prison and as a ruler of Egyptian economy.

Joseph said to him, "This is its interpretation: the three branches represent three days; within three days Pharaoh shall summon you, and restore you to your post, so that you shall place Pharaoh's cup in his hand as you used to do when you were his butler; if you will be good enough to keep me in mind when prosperity comes to you, do me the kindness of mentioning me to Pharaoh, and so liberate me from this house."

He (the king) restored the chief butler to his duties, so that he again placed the cup in Pharaoh's hand; but the chief baker he hanged, as Joseph had told them in his interpretation. Yet the chief butler did not remember Joseph. He forgot him.

—Genesis 40:12-14; 21-23

Joseph bought all the farm land of Egypt for Pharaoh, for every Egyptian sold his field, because the famine was so severe on them. Thus the land became Pharaoh's, and the people themselves he transferred to the towns from one end of Egypt's border to the other. It was only the priests' land that he did not buy; for the priests had an allotment from Pharaoh, and lived off the allotment which Pharaoh gave them; that was why they did not sell their land.

"Observe," said Joseph to the people, "that I have today bought you and your land for Pharaoh, here is seed for you to sow the land; a fifth of the crop you shall give to Pharaoh, and four-fifths shall go to yourselves for seed for the fields, and as food for your children." "You have saved our lives," they said. "We would be grateful to my lord; and we will become slaves to Pharaoh."

—Genesis 47:20-25

Then Joseph died, and all his brothers and all that generation. Then a new king ruled over Egypt who did not know Joseph.

—Exodus 1:6, 8

12. *I, Koheleth was King of Israel in Jerusalem.*

The use of the past tense "I was King" is interpreted by the Rabbis to mean that King Solomon was at one time deprived of his kingdom. This is another illustration of the instability of human success.

"I was somebody when I was King over Israel, but now I am nobody." Three worlds (turns of fortune) did Solomon experience in his lifetime. He was King, commoner and King; wise, foolish and again wise; rich, poor and again rich. What is the source? It is written, "I Koheleth, was King over Israel in Jerusalem."

—Midrash Rabbah, Ecclesiastes I

13. *I directed my heart to search and to explore with wisdom everything that happens beneath the Heavens. It is a sorry task that God has given men with which to occupy themselves.*

The author of this book of wisdom is not critical of wisdom in general. It is wisdom without any ethical or social purpose that he condemns.

Once a king married and permitted his wife access to all his treasures. He said to her, "All that I have is yours except this barrel which is full of scorpions." An old friend came to visit the queen and he inquired about the king's conduct. She told him that the king gave her all his treasures and left everything to her except one barrel of snakes. The friend said to her, "That is not so. Most of the king's treasures are in this barrel. He only told you this because he wants to marry another woman and give it all to her." So God had given Adam and Eve permission to eat of all the trees in the Garden of Eden except from the Tree of Knowledge of Good and Evil.

—Pirke D'reb Eliezer, Chapter 13

Adam and Eve disobeyed and ate of the Tree of Knowledge of Good and Evil. They tasted, enjoyed pure wisdom. Later generations rejected the concept that wisdom can be harmful. The use of atomic knowledge for destructive purposes and the misuse of scientific knowledge to annihilate human beings has proven the great danger of knowledge alone, of wisdom without morality. The story is told of a Nazi officer who was interrogating a Jew. With sadistic intention of frustrating the man in his clutches the Nazi said, "One eye of mine is artificial. It was set by the greatest German eye surgeon. No one can tell that there is a difference between my natural eye and the artificial one. If you can tell which is the artificial eye I shall set you free." The tired weak Jewish man lifted up his finger and pointed, "This is your artificial eye." Enraged the Nazi officer raved, "How did you know?" The answer was, "Your artificial eye is more human than your natural eye."

—J. S. S.

14. *I observed everything that happens under the sun and it seems that all is futile and a striving after wind.*

The author reports his observations. The Midrash transforms this pessimism into a warning.

An old man was sitting at the crossroads. Before him were two paths, one which was smooth at its beginning but with thorns, cedars and reeds at the far end; while the other road began with thorns, cedars and reeds and ended smoothly. The old man warned travelers on the road that the beginning of the first road might be smooth but it was snarled and tangled at the end; while the second one might be snarled and tangled at its beginning but it was smooth at the end. Ought not people be thankful to him for his warning that they should not tire themselves needlessly? So, too, should people be thankful to Solomon who sits by the gates of wisdom and warns Israel.

—Midrash Rabbah, Ecclesiastes I

15. *What is crooked cannot be made straight, what is missing cannot be counted.*

Observing nature, Koheleth surmises that that which is defective in nature is beyond human power to correct.

A bird made its nest on the edge of the sea and the sea swept the nest away. Then the bird said, "I will not move from here till I turn the dry land into sea and the sea into dry land." By what means? It took water from the sea in its mouth and poured it on the dry land and it took dust from the dry land and cast it into the sea. Another bird came and stood by and said: "Poor creature, with all your labor what can you change?"

—Midrash Rabbah, Esther 7

16. *I said to myself, "Indeed I have become great and acquired wisdom above all who preceded me in Jerusalem and my heart has perceived much wisdom and knowledge."*

The author is proud of his achievement, in acquiring much wisdom in a city famed for wisdom and where his predecessors were known as wise kings.

In Rome a lady of high rank asked Rabbi Yossi Ben Chalafta, "Why does the Book of Daniel say that God gives wisdom to the wise? Ought not God give wisdom to fools who need it?"

Let me answer your question with a parable. Two people wish to borrow money from you, one is rich and one is poor. To whom will you lend the money, to the rich man or to the poor man?"

She replied, "I would lend it to the rich man." "Why," he asked. "Because," she said, "if the rich man loses the money I lend him he will find some way to repay me. But if the poor man loses the money where will he get money to repay me?"

"Then apply your reasoning to the question of wisdom," said the Rabbi. "If God would bestow wisdom on the fools what do you think they would do with it? They would waste their wisdom in circuses, theatres and bath houses. But God gives wisdom to the wise who spend their time in meditation in synagogues and Houses of Study. Therefore He gives wisdom to the wise and knowledge to those who know understanding."

—Midrash Rabbah, Ecclesiastes I

17. *I directed my heart to knowing wisdom and to knowing madness and folly. I am convinced that this, too, is striving after wind.*

In his search to become wise he studied folly as well as wisdom. One can learn from every man.

They asked Rabbi Michal: "In the Ethics of the Fathers we read, Who is wise? He who learns from all men, as it is said: From all my teachers I have gotten understanding! Then why does it not answer, 'He who learns from every teacher.' " The Rabbi explained: "The sage who pronounced these words is intent on having it clear that we can learn

49

not only from those whose occupation it is to teach, but from every man. Even from one who is ignorant or from one who is wicked, you can gain understanding as to how to conduct your life."

—The Rabbi of Zlotchov

18. *For the more wisdom the more grief; and he who increases knowledge increases pain.*

The author closes this chapter on the search for wisdom with a realistic observation. The pursuit of wisdom has its dangers. Wisdom discovers that there are imperfections in both society and nature. This tends to increase frustration and unhappiness.

Four men entered the garden (of mystical knowledge). Who were they? Ben Azai, Ben Zoma, Acher (Elisha Ben Avuyah) and Rabbi Akiva. Rabbi Akiva said to them, "When you arrive at the stones of pure marble (knowledge) do not cry 'Water, water,' " thus implying that there are hazards in seeking this mystical wisdom. What were the effects of this increased knowledge upon them? Ben Azai entered and died. Ben Zoma entered and lost his mind. Acher entered, distorted the knowledge and became a heretic. Rabbi Akiva alone entered and departed unhurt.

—Talmud, Chagiga p. 14b

CHAPTER TWO

1. *I said to myself, "Come now, I will test you with pleasure and have a good time." But this too turned out to be futile.*

The Midrash and many commentators interpret this verse to refer to indulgence in wine.

After the flood Noah began planting. Satan came to him and asked, "What are you planting here?"

Noah answered, "I am planting a vineyard."

"And what fruit will it yield?"

"Delicious grapes to make wine, which gladdens the heart."

"Then let us work together," said Satan. Noah agreed. Satan then brought a lamb, slaughtered it and poured its blood on the ground. He brought a lion, slaughtered it and poured its blood on the soil. He did the same with an ape and a pig. He slaughtered them and fertilized the earth with their blood. What did Satan want to indicate to Noah? When a man drinks the first cup of wine, he becomes mild and meek like a lamb. After the second cup, he becomes daring as a lion, boasting of his power and his might. After the third and fourth cups he becomes like an ape, dances, leaps and makes a fool of himself. When he drinks even more he is like a pig, bestial, filthy and wallowing in the mud.

—Midrash Tanchuma, Noah 13

2. *Of merrymaking I concluded, "It is folly" and of pleasure, "What does it accomplish?"*

There is a pleasant and painful side to life. It is unwise for one to base his life on pleasure alone since even innocent pleasure is ephemeral and passing.

The son of an eminent man of Babylon married. His father made a dinner for the sages and said to his son, "Go up to the attic and bring us some good wine from a special cask." He went up to the attic where a serpent bit him and he died. The father waited for him to come back. When he failed to do so, the father went up and found his son had been bitten by the serpent and was lying dead among the casks. The pious man waited there until his guests had eaten all their meal and were about to say the Grace after meals. Then he came down, and spoke to them, "My masters, not to say blessings for the bridegroom have you come to my house; rather, say over him a benediction for mourners. Not to conduct him under the marriage canopy have you come; convey him to the grave." Rabbi Zakkai delivered the funeral oration over him on the text, "Of merrymaking I concluded 'It is folly' and of pleasure 'What does it accomplish?' "

—Midrash Rabbah, Ecclesiastes II

3. *I resolved in my heart to indulge my body with wine while my mind was acting with wisdom and grasping folly, until I might discover what course is best for men to follow in their brief span of life under Heaven.*

Man has a potential for good and evil, therefore indulgence in pleasure as well as the pursuit of wisdom are both to be explored. The author attempts to find which is the best path in life.

Man contains within himself all the worlds that exist. He is therefore able to have contact with them all. Man possesses within himself all good and all evil traits, but they are in an unborn state. It is within his power to give them birth. If he is angelic in character, he will transform evil traits into good. If he is demonic, he will transform good traits into evil. It is the study of Torah that aids us to become good.

—The Rabbi of Koretz

4. I extended my enterprises, I built mansions for myself and I planted vineyards for myself.

The author carries out his plan for the indulgence in pleasure by building a series of magnificent mansions.

Solomon was building his own house thirteen years until he had finished his entire house. He also built the Forest of Lebanon House; its length was one hundred cubits, and its breadth fifty cubits, and its height thirty cubits, upon four rows of cedar pillars, with cedar beams upon the pillars.

It was covered above with cedar over the forty-five beams that were upon the columns, and the number of the pillars was fifteen in a row. There were also window frames in three rows, and the window was over against window in three tiers. All the doors and posts had square frames; and door was over against door in three tiers. He also made the pillared porch fifty cubits long and thirty cubits broad, and a porch in front of them and columns and a cornice in front of them. And he made the porch of the throne where he might judge, even the Porch of Judgment; and it was covered with cedar from floor to rafters.

His own house, where he was to dwell, belonging to another court farther back from the Porch was of like workmanship. He also made a house for Pharaoh's daughter. All these were of costly stones, hewn according to measurements, sawed with saws, within and without, even from the foundation to the coping, and from the outside to the great court. The foundation also was of costly, great stones, stones of ten cubits and stones of eight cubits. Above were costly stones, hewn according to measurement, as well as cedar.

The great encircling court had three rows of hewn stones and a row of cedar beams, as in the case of the inner court of the house of the Lord and the court of the porch of the house.

—I Kings 7:1-13

So Solomon rebuilt Gezer, lower Beth-horon, Baalath, and Tadmar in the desert land. All the store-cities that Solomon had, cities for his chariots, the cities for his horsemen, and whatsoever Solomon desired he built in Jerusalem, in Lebanon, and in all the lands under his rule.

—I Kings 9:17-19

Pharaoh's daughter went up from the city of David to her own house which he had built for her, then he built Millo.

—I Kings 9:24

5. *I laid out gardens and orchards and I planted in them all kinds of fruit trees.*

As part of his plan for material enjoyment he beautified his physical surroundings by planting of delicate fruit trees and ornamental gardens.

Solomon had a vineyard at Baalhamon; he gave over the vineyard to caretakers. Each would bring in a thousand silver pieces for its fruit. I keep my vineyard to myself; you, Solomon, are welcome to the thousand shekels, and the caretakers of the fruit to the two hundred shekels. O you who sit in the gardens, the companions are listening to your voice; let me hear it too! Hurry, my beloved, swift as a gazelle, or like a young deer, on the mountain of spices.

—Song of Songs 8:11-19

When King Solomon built the Holy Temple, he planted
therein all kinds of (trees of) golden delights, which brought
forth their fruits in their season, and as the winds blew upon
them, they would fall off, as the Psalmist sings: "May his
fruits rustle like Lebanon." (Psalms 72-16) When the for-
eigners entered the Temple they withered as the Prophet
Nahum (1:4) declares: "And the flower of Lebanon will
fade." The Holy One, blessed be He, will restore them in
the future. "It shall blossom abundantly and rejoice, even
with joy and singing; the glory of Lebanon shall be given
unto it." (Isaiah 35-2)

—Talmud, Yoma p. 21b

6. *I constructed pools of water to irrigate the forest of
sprouting trees.*

The young and tender trees in his gardens could not depend on the rainfall which was frequently insufficient.
In an arid country there was always a need for extra
water from wells and cisterns as these references from
various Biblical periods show.

When Hezekiah saw that Sennacherib had come determined
to attack Jerusalem, he decided in council with his princes
and his leading men to stop the water of the fountains that
were outside the city, and they helped him. Indeed a great
crowd of people gathered and stopped up all the fountains
and the torrent that coursed through the midst of the land
saying, "Why should the kings of Assyria come and find
abundant water?"

—II Chronicles 32:2, 3, 4

Then the king of Assyria sent the commander-in-chief,
and the chief of the Eunuchs and the field marshal from
Lachish with a large army against King Hezekiah at Jerusalem, they came and took up their position by the conduit

of the upper pool, which is on the highway to the laundry-men's fields.

—II Kings 18:17

Then said the Lord to Isaiah, "Go out now to meet Ahaz, you and your son Shaar-Yeshuv, at the end of the aque-duct from the upper pool, on the highway to the laundry-men's field; and say to him, Take care, and keep calm."

—Isaiah 7:3

You saw the breakers of the city of David that were many and you gathered together the waters of the lower pool. You also counted the houses of Jerusalem, and broke down the houses to fortify the wall; and you made a reser-voir between the two walls for the waters of the old pool. But you looked not to him who brought it about, nor paid attention to him who planted it long ago.

—Isaiah 22:9-11

Shallum, the son of Colhozehm the ruler of the district of Mitzpeh, repaired the Fountain Gate Shelach. He built it and covered it, and set up its doors, its bolts, and its bars. He also built the wall of the pool of Siloam near the king's garden, even to the stairs that go down from the city of David.

—Nehemiah 3:15, 16

7. *I acquired male and female slaves and I had house-born servants. I also owned much cattle and sheep, more than anyone who preceded me in Jerusalem.*

For the maintenance of the palaces and gardens Solomon required countless servants. In turn, to feed this huge staff there was a need for large provisions.

Solomon's provision for one day was thirty kors of fine flour, and sixty kors of meal, ten fat oxen and twenty pasture fed oxen and a hundred sheep, besides harts and gazelles and roebucks and fatted fowls. Now Solomon had forty thousand stalls of horses for his chariots, and twelve thousand horsemen. These officers supplied provisions for King Solomon and for all who came to King Solomon's table, each man in his month. They fell short in nothing. Also barley and straw for the horses and the swift steeds they brought to the place where it should be, each man according to his assignment.

—I Kings 5:2, 3; 6-8

8. *I collected for myself silver and gold and the treasures of kings and provinces. I obtained for myself male and female singers, man's delights, coaches and chariots.*

Kings and queens admired the wealth and elegance of King Solomon. For his own pleasure and for the entertainment of his guests he acquired (musical talent) and various luxuries.

The weight of gold that came to Solomon in one year was six hundred and sixty-six talents of gold, besides what came from the traffic of the merchants and spice dealers and from all the kings of the Arabs and from the governors of the land.

Now King Solomon made two hundred large shields of beaten gold (six hundred shekels of gold going into each shield). He made three hundred shields of beaten gold (three manas of gold going into each shield), and the king put them in the Palace called the Forest of Lebanon. The king also had six steps and at the top of the throne were calves' heads, and on both sides of the seat were arms, and two lions stood beside the arms. Twelve lions stood there on the six steps on each side. The like was never made in any kingdom.

All the drinking vessels of King Solomon were of gold, and all the vessels of the House of the Forest of Lebanon were of rare gold; none were of silver, since it was thought of as nothing in the days of Solomon.

For the king had at sea a fleet of Tarshish ships with the fleet of Hiram. Once every three years the fleet of Tarshish ships used to come bringing gold, sliver, ivory, apes and peacocks.

King Solomon excelled all the kings of the earth in riches and wisdom. The whole earth sought the presence of Solomon to hear the wisdom which God had put into his mind. They brought each his present: vessels of silver and gold, clothing, equipment, spices, horses and mules, so much year by year. Moreover Solomon gathered together chariots and horsemen; and he had fourteen hundred chariots and twelve thousand horsemen, that he stationed in Jerusalem. The king made silver in Jerusalem as common as stone, and he made cedars as plentiful as the sycamore trees that are in the lowland.

—I Kings 10:14-27

9. *So I became great and surpassed all my predecessors in Jerusalem. Indeed, my wisdom stood by me.*

The author states that he surpassed his predecessors both in wisdom and wealth. He attributes the acquisition of his material resources to his wisdom.

An officer became great in the royal palace. The king said to him, "Ask what you want and I shall give it to you." The officer thought to himself, "If I ask for silver and gold, pearls or garments, he will give them to me; but I will ask for his daughter in marriage and then everything will be given to me." So too, in Gibeon the Lord appeared to Solomon in a dream by night; and God said: "Ask what I shall give you." (I Kings III, 5) Solomon thought to himself, "If I ask for silver and gold and pearls, He will give them to me; but I shall ask for wisdom and then everything will be included." That was Solomon's prayer.

—Midrash Rabbah, Ecclesiastes I

10. *I did not withhold anything that my eyes desired, I did not deny myself any pleasure for my heart rejoiced in all my labor; and this was my reward for all my effort.*

Here the author applies his formula to find happiness by plunging into a life of pleasure and indulgence. The Rabbis of the Midrash use this text as an occasion to speculate on the extremes of an elegant cuisine.

A woman took her son to a baker in Caesarea and said to him, "Teach my son the occupation." He replied to her, "Let him stay with me five years and I will teach him five hundred recipes with wheat." He stayed with the master baker five years and was taught five hundred recipes with wheat. The baker said to the mother of the apprentice, "Let him stay with me another five years and I will teach him a thousand recipes with wheat."

But how many recipes are possible with wheat? Rabbi Chanina and Rabbi Jonathan were both sitting and reckoning (how many ways were there of baking wheat) and stopped at sixty. Rabbi Eleazar then told another tale in the name of Rabbi Yossi. A woman of Caesarea once took her son to a cook and said to him, "Teach my son the occupation." He replied to her, "Let him stay with me for four years and I will teach him a hundred foods made from eggs."

He stayed with him four years and was taught a hundred foods made from eggs. The cook said to her, "Let him stay with me another four years and I will teach him another hundred dishes made from eggs." Rabbi Judah the Prince heard this and exclaimed: "We do not know what good living is!"

—Midrash Rabbah, Ecclesiastes I

11. *Then I examined all the accomplishments that my hands had built up and the possessions that I toiled to acquire, and all seemed futile and striving after wind. And there is no gain under the sun.*

He now pauses to evaluate the pursuit of pleasure and the amassing of material possessions. He finds them meaningless. They do not make life worth living.

Rabbi Levi said: "This may be likened to a bird kept in a cage. Another bird came, and said to it, 'Happy are you, for your food is provided for you!' The caged bird replied, 'You consider my food but pay no attention to my being shut up; tomorrow they will take me out and slay me!'"

—Midrash Rabbah, Ecclesiastes XI

12. *I then turned to observe wisdom, hilarity, and folly; for what can the man do who comes after the king? That which he has already done!*

Solomon, with all the power at his disposal has searched and reached certain conclusions. He wonders what a man with limited means can discover? The following Midrash cites four examples of great men who by reason of their expertise and experience reached certain conclusions.

King Solomon said: "Vanity of vanities, all is vanity." (Ecclesiastes 1:2) If another had made such declaration, I might have said that this man, who never owned two pennies in his life, makes light of the world's wealth. But for Solomon, of whom the Bible tells, "And the King made silver to be in Jerusalem as stones," (I Kings 10:27) for him it is fitting to conclude "Vanity of Vanities, all is vanity."

King Nebuchadnezzar said, "And all the inhabitants of the earth are reputed as nothing." (Daniel 4:32) If any other man had made such a pronouncement. I might have said that this man, who never ruled over two flies, thinks of inhabitants as nothing. But it was fitting for the wicked King Nebuchadnezzar who ruled the world to say so. (Daniel 2:38)

Jethro said, "Now I know that the Lord is greater than all Gods." (Exodus 18:11) If any other wise man of the heathen people expressed such words, I might have said that this man, who does not understand the real nature of idolatry, makes such declaration. But for Jethro, concerning whom Rabbi Yishmoel taught that Jethro did not omit a single form of idolatry in the world without serving it, it was fitting for him to declare, "Now I know that the Lord is greater than all the Gods."

Moses said: "The Rock, His work is perfect." (Deuteronomy 32:4) If another prophet and sage had stood up to declare, "The Rock, His work is perfect," one might have said, How does he know? But it was appropriate for Moses our teacher to declare it since it is written of him, "He made known His ways unto Moses, His doings unto the children of Israel." (Psalms 103:7)

—Midrash Rabbah, Ecclesiastes 3:11

13. *Then I perceived that wisdom excels folly as light excels darkness.*

The experiment with wisdom and folly revealed one definite result—that there is a distinct advantage in wisdom over folly.

Rabbi Yossi ben Kisma said: Once walking on the road a man met me and greeted me, and I returned his greeting. He said to me: "Rabbi, from what city are you?" I told him: "I come from a great city of sages and scholars." He said to me, "Rabbi, are you willing to live with us in our city?" I told him: "Were you to give me all the silver and gold and all precious stones and pearls in the world, I would not live anywhere except in a place of Torah."

61

So too, it is written in the Book of Psalms by David King of Israel: "Thy own teaching means more to me than thousands in gold and silver." For, when a man dies, neither silver nor gold nor precious stones nor pearls accompany him, but Torah and good deeds alone, as it is said: "When you walk, it shall guide you; when you lie down, it shall watch over you; and when you awake, it shall talk with you." When you walk, it shall guide you in this world; when you lie down, it shall watch over you in the grave; and when you awake, it shall talk to you in the world to come. It also says: "Mine is the silver and mine is the gold, says the Lord of hosts."

—Ethics of the Fathers 6:9

14. *The wise man has his eyes in his head but the fool walks in darkness; but I also realized that the same fate overtakes them all.*

The wise man has eyes in his head.

When the Holy One, blessed be He, said to him, "Abraham, take your son, your only son," (Genesis 22:2) he went on the journey. On the first day and on the second day he saw nothing. What of the third day? "He saw the place in the distance." (ib. 4) What did he see? He saw a cloud over the mountain and said, "I think this is the mountain upon which the Holy One, blessed be He, has told me to offer my son Isaac." Abraham said to Isaac, "Isaac, my son, do you see what I see?" He answered, "Yes." "What do you see?" he asked, and Isaac replied, "A cloud over the mountain." Abraham asked Eliezer and Ishmael, his young men, "Do you see anything?" They answered, "No." He said, "Since you see nothing and the ass sees nothing, stay here with the ass because you are people insensitive as the ass."

—Midrash Rabbah, Ecclesiastes IX

15. *Then I reflected in my heart. Since what may happen to the fool will also happen to me, of what use was it then for me to have become so extremely wise? And I concluded that this too is futility.*

This sentence is pervaded by a sense of the ultimate fate of man, death. The fool will die and so will I. Then "of what use" were my efforts to attain wisdom.

The ministering angels asked the Holy One, blessed be He: "Sovereign of the Universe! Why did You impose the penalty of death upon Adam?" He said to them, "I gave him one easy command, yet he violated it." "But," protested the angels, "Moses and Aaron fulfilled the whole Torah, yet they died." To which came the sincere answer: "There is one event to the righteous and to the wicked." (Dying is the end of every man.)

—Talmud, Sabbath p. 55b

16. *For the wise man is no more remembered forever than the fool; in the days to come all will be forgotten. How the wise man dies just like the fool!*

In the days to come all will be forgotten.

A company of tourists had travelled together for a long time in several carriages. One broke down and they found it could no longer continue the trip. The stranded travellers asked those about to continue the trip to remember them and to send relief. On reaching the city these tourists forgot their fellow travellers.

—Dubno Maggid

17. *So I was disgusted with life. For I was depressed by all that goes on under the sun, because all seems futile and a striving after wind.*

I was disgusted with life.

"Why is light given to the wretched, and life to the bitter in soul; who long for death, but it comes not, and hunt for it more than for buried treasures, those who would rejoice exultingly, and would be glad, if they could find the grave? To a man whose way is hidden, whom God has fenced in? For my sighing comes instead of my food, and my groans are poured forth like water. If I entertain a fear, then it comes upon me; and what I was afraid of befalls me. I was not at ease, nor was I quiet, nor had I rest; but trouble came."

—Job 3:20-26

18. *And I detested all my wealth which I had achieved under the sun, for I must leave it to the man who will succeed me.*

For I must leave it to the man who will succeed me.

Why is mankind compared to a weasel. It is because a weasel gathers and then leaves what she has collected and she does not know for whom she leaves it. So also human beings accumulate and leave, accumulate and leave, not knowing for whom they are leaving. The Psalmist says, "He heaps up riches and knows not who will gather them." (Psalm 39:7)

—Jerusalem Talmud, Sabbath Chapter 14:1

19. *And who knows whether he will be a wise man or a fool? Yet he will control all my possessions for which I exerted toil and exercised wisdom under the sun. This also is futility.*

And who knows whether he will be a wise man or a fool?

A wealthy man from Jerusalem travelled on business. In one city he became fatally sick. Before he died, he told his host that he was willing to entrust him his possessions. "In time my son will come here from Jerusalem. You will recognize

64

him by three clever things he will do. Then you must give him all my money and all my belongings." As months passed and the father did not return to Jerusalem the son travelled to that distant city to search for his father.

The son knew the name of the host in whose house his father stayed. As soon as he arrived in the city he looked for that house. Where ever he would ask for the whereabouts of the local merchant, the answer would be, "I don't know." For the host had asked his townspeople not to divulge his address to any stranger. The son finally thought of a plan. He saw a woodcutter carrying a load of wood. "I would like to buy your wood." They agreed on a price and he paid him for the wood. Then he told him, "This wood is to be delivered to the house of this man," and he mentioned the name of the merchant he was looking for.

The woodcutter went to deliver the wood, but a little distance behind him walked the young man from Jerusalem.

When the woodcutter reached the house, he called the owner by name, "Come and get your wood." "Wood? What wood? I never ordered any wood from you!" "Maybe you did not, but this young man did. He paid for it and asked me to deliver it to you." Surprised, the merchant invited the young man into his house and asked him who he was. "I am the son of the man who lodged here and failed to return home."

In the evening at dinner the host asked the son to honor them by serving. On the table were five roasted pigeons. He gave one pigeon to his host and his wife. One pigeon he gave to the man's two sons and one pigeon he gave to the two daughters. For himself he kept two pigeons.

At the next meal they had stuffed chicken. Once again the host asked the stranger to serve. He accepted the honor. He gave the head of the fowl to the host, the heart and the liver to the hostess, the legs to the sons and the wings to the daughters. For himself he kept the body. The host asked for an explanation for this behavior. "I will explain to you what I did. At the first meal I had to serve five roasted pigeons. I gave you and your wife one pigeon for together you were three. Your two sons and one pigeon and your two daughters and one pigeon all numbered three. To keep the number just as equal I had to take the remaining two pigeons for myself. On serving the chicken, because you are the head of the house, I gave you the head. I gave the inside to your wife because from within her came your children. Your sons are the pillars of your household, I gave them the legs. To your daughters I gave the wings for in due time they will fly away from you with husbands. For myself, I kept the body, which has the shape of a boat, for tomorrow I am sailing home."

"The Lord be praised," said the host, "you are truly the son of your father, for I know you by the three clever things you have done, first with the wood, second with the roasted pigeons and then with the chicken." Then he returned to the son the entire fortune of his father.

—Midrash, Lamentations 1:3

20. *I turned to view with despair all the gains for which I toiled under the sun.*

> The Midrash comments that the author reconsidered his despair and said, "Just as others toil for me, so I must toil for others."

Emperor Hadrian was walking along the roads of Tiberias. He saw an old man cutting down shrubs to set plants. He said to him, "Old man, old man, how old are you?" He answered, "I am a hundred." The king said to him, "You are a hundred years old, and you stand cutting shrubs to set plants! Do you think you will eat of their fruit?" He replied, "If I am worthy, I shall eat; if not, just as my forefathers toiled for me, so I toil for my children." The Emperor told him, "By your life, if you are fortunate enough to eat of their fruit, let me know." Later on the plantings produced figs, and the old man said, "Now is the time to inform the king." What did he do? He filled a basket with figs, and went up to the palace gate. He was asked, "What do you want?" He said to them, "Go and tell the king, an old Jew whom you once met wishes to greet you." The Emperor heard and said, "Bring him in." When he entered, the king asked, "What do you want?" He replied, "I am the old man whom you met when I was cutting shrubs to set plants, and you said to me that if I was fortunate enough to eat of the fruits I should inform you. Behold, I have been worthy to eat of them and these figs are the fruit they produced."

Hadrian thereupon said, "I order that his basket be emptied of the figs and filled with golden coins." His attendant asked him, "You show all this honor to this old Jew?" Hadrian answered, "His Creator has honored him, so will I."

—Midrash Rabbah, Ecclesiastes II

21. *For here is a man who has labored with wisdom, intelligence and success and yet must leave his property to a man who has not toiled for it. This, too, is futility and a great misfortune.*

> Here the author expresses regret over having to leave the possessions he amassed to one who has not worked for it. Then too, there is an implied regret that the one who will inherit this fortune will not guard it with the same zeal as he who had to work for it.

A man is held responsible for everything he receives in the world and his children are responsible, too. Let not a person who inherits from his father or mother think, "This wealth is my inheritance. I can do with what I please." The fact is, nothing belongs to him, everything is the Lord's, and whatever he has received, he has received only on credit and the Lord will exact payment for it. This may be compared to a person who entered a city and found no one there. He walked into a house and there found a table set with all

67

kinds of food and drink. He began to eat and drink, thinking "I deserve all this. All of it is mine. I shall do with it what I please." He didn't even notice that the owners were watching him from the side! He had yet to pay for everything he ate and drank, for he was in a spot from which he was not able to escape.

—Rabbainu Yonah

22. *For what has a man of all his labor and of the striving of his heart for which he toils under the sun?*

For what has a man of all his labor.

The impulse which drives a man on and on is like a boy who teases his friends by asking them to guess what he has in the closed palm of his hand. Each friend guesses that the closed palm conceals whatever is particularly desirable to himself. When the hand is opened you will find it contains nothing.

—The Rabbi of Bratzlav

23. *For all his days are painful and his business provoking and even at night his mind has no rest. This too is vanity.*

Men often carry unnecessary burdens. Their schemes disturb their composure at daytime and deprive them of their sleep by night.

A man carrying a heavy bundle was offered a ride by someone driving by in a wagon. As they were riding, the wagon owner noticed that his passenger was still holding his heavy load upon his shoulders. The host asked his passenger, "Why don't you put your heavy pack down on the floor?" The passenger answered, "You have been kind enough to give me a lift. Why should you have the added burden of my package?"

—Dubno Maggid

24. *There is nothing better for man but that he eat and drink and find satisfaction in his work. This, also, I perceive is a gift of God.*

A gift of God.

Rabbi (Yehuda the Prince) asked Rabbi Yishmoel, son of Rabbi Yossi, "What is the reason that the rich in the Land of Israel deserve wealth?" He answered, "Because they give tithes." "Why are those in Babylonia deserving of wealth?" "Because they honor the Torah." "And those in other countries? Why do they merit wealth?" "Because they honor the Sabbath."

Rabbi Cheyah ben Abba related this story: Once I was a guest of a man in the city of Ludkia at dinner, sixteen men carried in a gold table. On it were silver chains, plates, goblets and pitchers filled with all kinds of food, dainties and spices. When they sat down they recited, "The earth is the Lord's and the fullness thereof." When they removed all at the end of the meal, they recited, "The heaven is the Lord's heaven but the earth He has given to mankind." I said to my host, "Tell me how did you merit all this?" He replied, "I was a butcher, and of every fine cattle I used to say, "This shall be for the Sabbath day." I told him, "Happy are you that you have merited this and praised be the Almighty who has permitted you to enjoy all this."

—Talmud, Sabbath p. 119a

25. *For who should eat and who enjoy, except I?*

For who should eat and who enjoy.

Rabbi Yishmoel, who was as much distinguished by the greatness of his mind as by his large physique, visited Reb Shimon. Reb Shimon received his guest cordially, discussing learned subjects with him.

The host filled a cup of wine and handed it to his guest who took it and drank it down at one time. "My friend,

Yishmoel," said the host, "do you remember what our sages said on this subject, that one who drinks his goblet in one gulp is greedy?" "I well remember," said Rabbi Yishmoel, "the saying of our teachers that people ought not to drink a full cup of wine at once. The wise men have not stated their rule so as to allow of no exception. And in this instance there are three exceptions: the cup is small, the recipient is large and your wine delicious."

—Talmud, Pesochin p. 86b

26. *He grants wisdom, knowledge and happiness to the person who pleases Him, but to the sinner He assigns the task of gathering and amassing so that he may leave it to one who is pleasing to God. This also is vanity and striving after wind.*

> In the closing sentence of this chapter the author makes the positive statement that there is design and direction in life, controlled by God. Even if the sinner amasses wealth it will in time come into the ownership of one who is pleasing to God.

A wealthy man owned a large business as well as the only restaurant and bar in his city. This man had two sons. One was serious and sensible and helped his father in all his activities. The other was a playboy, a drunkard and a spendthrift. When the father grew old he made a will leaving his commercial business to the younger son, the playboy, and to his older son he left the restaurant and bar. Friends asked the father, "How is it that you leave the bulk of your business to your son who does not appreciate the value of money and your decent son you leave only the restaurant and bar?"

The father's explanation was this: "If I were to leave the restaurant and bar to my younger son, in no time he and his friends would eat and drink and ruin the business. In the end the creditors would take the restaurant. That is why the restaurant and bar I left to my wise son and the general business to my foolish son.

"Since there is no other bar in the city, where will my younger son go to spend his fortune with his drunken friends? They will have to go to my older son. There he will spend his money and eventually his inherited fortune. Then the wise son will ultimately have both portions of the inheritance."

—Dubno Maggid

CHAPTER THREE

1. *For everything there is a season and a time for every experience under heaven.*

A time for every experience.

There was a time for Adam to enter the Garden of Eden, as the Bible relates: "The Lord God took the man and placed him into the Garden of Eden. (Genesis 2:15) And there was a time for him to leave it, as told in Genesis 3:23: "Therefore the Lord God banished him from the Garden of Eden." There was a time for Noah to enter the ark, when God commanded, "Enter the ark with all your household (Genesis 7:1); and a time for him to leave the ark, when God ordered him, "Come out from the ark." (Genesis 8:16) There was a time for the Torah to be given to Israel. Rabbi Bibi said: There was a time for a precious object to be found above the heaven and now it is to be found beneath the heaven. What was it? The Torah, as the Bible tells, "And God spoke all these words," (Exodus 20:1) on giving the ten commandments on Mount Sinai.

—Midrash Rabbah, Ecclesiastes III

2. *A time to be born and a time to die; a time to plant and a time to uproot what is planted.*

A time to be born.

Amram, the father of Moses was the greatest man of his generation. When he saw that the wicked Pharaoh had decreed, "Every son that is born ye shall throw into the river," he said, "In vain do we labor." He divorced his wife. All (the Israelites) divorced their wives. His daughter, Miriam, said to him, "Father, your decree is more severe than Pharaoh's. Pharaoh decreed death only against the male children whereas you have decreed against male and female. Pharaoh only decreed concerning this world whereas you have decreed regarding this world and the world to come. In the case of the wicked Pharaoh there is some doubt whether his decree will be fulfilled, whereas in your case, because you are righteous, it is certain that your decree will be fulfilled, as it is written 'You shall also make a decree and it shall be established unto you.'" He then took his wife back and they all took their wives back.

—Talmud, Sotah p. 12a

A time to die.

Rabbi Jochanan said: "A man's feet are responsible for him. They lead him to the place where he is wanted."

There were two Ethiopian men, Elihoreph and Ahyoh, who were scribes of King Solomon. One day Solomon observed that the Angel of Death seemed sad. "Why are you sad?" asked Solomon. "Because," answered the Angel of Death, "Heaven decreed that I take the two Ethiopians who sit there." Solomon, to save them from death, sent them to the city of Luz. When they reached the gates of Luz they died. The next day Solomon saw the Angel of Death and he was cheerful. "Why?" Solomon asked, "are you so cheerful?" The Angel replied, "Because you sent the men to the very place where it was destined that they should die." Solomon uttered the saying, "A man's feet are responsible for him. They lead him to the place where he is wanted."

—Talmud, Sukah p. 53a

3. *A time to kill and a time to heal; a time to break down and a time to build up.*

A time to break down and a time to build up.

The earth became corrupt before God; the earth was filled with lawlessness. God saw that the earth was corrupt for all living on earth had corrupted its ways. God said to Noah, "I have decided to put an end to all living beings, for the earth is filled with lawlessness because of them; I am about to destroy them with the earth. Make yourself an ark of gopher wood; make it an ark with compartments, and cover it inside and out with pitch. This is how you are to make it: the length of the ark is to be three hundred cubits, its width fifty cubits, and its height thirty cubits. Make an opening for daylight in the ark, finishing it off on top to the width of a cubit. Put the entrance to the ark in its side; make it with lower, second, and third decks.

"For my part, I am about to bring a flood of water upon the earth, to destroy all flesh under the heavens in whom there is breath of life; everything on earth shall perish.

"But I will establish My covenant with you, and you shall enter the ark, with your sons, your wife and your sons' wives. And of all that lives, of all flesh, you shall take two of each into the ark to keep alive with you; they shall be male and female.

"Of the various kinds of birds, the various kinds of cattle, and of every kind of creeping thing on earth, two of each shall come to you to stay alive. For your part, take all edible food that is eaten and store it away, to serve as food for you and them." Noah did so; he did just as God commanded him.

—Genesis 6:11-22

4. *A time to cry and a time to laugh; a time to mourn and a time to dance.*

A time to cry and a time to laugh.

Rabbi Gamliel, Rabbi Eliezer, Rabbi Joshua and Rabbi Akiva were coming to Jerusalem after the destruction of Jerusalem and the Temple.

Just as they reached Mt. Scopus they saw a fox emerge from the Holy of Holies. They all began weeping except Rabbi Akiva who was cheerful. They asked him "Why are you cheerful?" Rabbi Akiva asked, "Why are you weeping?" They answered, "The Temple site of which it is said, 'And the stranger who draws near shall be put to death' has now become a hunting ground for foxes and should we not weep?"

"For that reason, I am cheerful," he answered. "It it written in Isaiah (8:2), 'I will take to me trusted witnesses to record, Uriah the priest and Zechariah the son of Jeberechia.' Now what connection is there between Uriah the priest and Zechariah? Uriah lived during the times of the first temple while Zechariah lived during the second Temple but Scripture linked the later prophecy with the earlier prophecy of Uriah. In the earlier prophecy of Uriah it is written 'Therefore, Zion shall be ploughed as a field.' In the book of Zechariah it is written 'Thus says the Lord of Hosts, aged men and women shall again dwell in the streets of Jerusalem.' So long as Uriah's prophecy of destruction had not been fulfilled, I had misgivings lest Zechariah's prophecy might not be fulfilled. Now that the prophecy of Uriah has been fulfilled it is certain that Zecheriah's prophecy will also find its literal fulfillment. The Rabbis said to him, 'Akiva, you have comforted us, Akiva you have comforted us.' "

—Talmud, Makkoth p. 24b

5. *A time to scatter stones and a time to gather stones; a time to embrace and a time to refrain from embracing.*

A time to embrace and a time to refrain from embracing.

But Naomi said to her daughters-in-law, "Go, return each of you to her mother's house. May the Lord deal as kindly with you, as you have dealt with the dead and with me! May the Lord grant that each of you find security in the house of a husband!" Then she kissed them. They broke into weeping and said to her, "No, we will return with you to your people."

But Naomi replied, "Turn back, my daughters! Why should you go with me? Have I any more sons in my body who might be husbands for you? Return, my daughters, go, for I am too old to be married. Even if I thought there was hope for me, even if I were married tonight and I also bore sons, would you wait for them to grow up? Would you forego marriage for them? No, my daughters! My lot is far more bitter than yours, for the hand of the Lord has been raised against me."

They broke into weeping again, and Orpha kissed her mother-in-law good-by, but Ruth clung to her. So she said, "See, your sister-in-law has returned to her people and her gods. Go follow your sister-in-law."

But Ruth replied, "Do not urge me to leave you, to turn back and not follow you. For wherever you go, I will go; wherever you lodge, I will lodge; your people shall be my people, and your God, my God. Where you die, I will die, and there I will be buried. Thus and more may the Lord do to me if anything but death parts me from you."

When Naomi saw how determined she was to go with her, she ceased to argue with her and the two went on until they reached Bethlehem.

—Ruth 1:8-19

6. *A time to seek and a time to lose; a time to guard and a time to discard.*

A time to discard.

A merchant once made a voyage with his son taking with him chests filled with gold. The captain assigned to them quarters in a dark part of the ship. The merchant overheard the voices of the sailors saying, "When we are out on the high sea, we will kill them, throw them overboard and take their money." What did this merchant do?

He pretended to quarrel with his son and took the chests and threw them into the sea in the presence of the sailors. When they reached port the merchant went and charged the sailors before the court of the emperor who imprisoned the sailors and ordered them to compensate the merchant for the loss of money.

The captain said to the Judge, "How do you judge us to be guilty?" He answered them with King Solomon's adage that there is "A time to discard." To save his life the man had been compelled to throw his money overboard and the scheming sailors were responsible for his loss.

—Midrash Rabbah, Ecclesiastes III

7. *A time to rend and a time to mend; a time to be silent and a time to speak.*

A time to be silent and a time to speak.

A fable tells of a wise man watching a person talking more than listening. He said to that person, "Observe the difference between your ears and your mouth. God created for you two ears and one mouth so that you would listen twice as much as you speak."

—Rabbi Joseph Nachmies

8. *A time to love and a time to hate; a time for war and a time for peace.*

A time to love and a time to hate.

There are three whom God loves: one who does not display

anger, one who does not become intoxicated, and one who does not insist on retaliation.

There are three God hates: he who says one thing with his mouth and another with his heart, he who has evidence about his neighbor and does not testify for him, and he who observes an indecent act of his neighbor and testifies against him alone (insufficient testimony).

It happened that a man named Tobias sinned and a man, Zigud, alone came and testified against him before Rabbi Papa. The Rabbi had Zigud punished. Zigud complained, "Tobias sinned and Zigud is punished?"

"Yes," was the answer, "for it is written, 'One witness shall not rise up against a man.' (Two witnesses are needed for conviction.) Since you have testified against him alone, you merely caused an ill reputation."

—Talmud, Pesochim p. 113b

9. *What does the worker gain by his effort?*

In the preceding sentences the author teaches that everything in life is pre-ordained, "that there is a time for every experience." If life is governed and controlled, man should realize his is a minimal contribution.

A blind man was a guest at a large party. It was an elaborate feast. Every time a fellow guest seated next to him offered him some food, the blind man would bless him for his kindness. The blind man mistook his fellow guest for the host.

At the end of the meal someone told the blind man that he was expressing gratitude for the invitation and the meal to a fellow guest. "You better express your thanks to the host," he was admonished. So it is in the life of man; he should consider who is the real source of his sustenance.

—Dubno Maggid

10. *I have considered the task which God has given to men to occupy themselves with.*

To occupy themselves.

This is the peculiarity of amassing wealth. Rabbi Judah said in the name of Rabbi Aibu: No one departs from the world with even half his desire gratified. If he has a hundred he wants to turn it into two hundred. If he has two hundred he wants to turn them into four hundred.

—Midrash Rabbah, Ecclesiastes 3:10

11. *He has made everything properly in its time; He also put eternity in their hearts, but man can never comprehend the plan of God's work in its entirety.*

The sentence begins with a positive affirmation of divine rule. Although man may understand fragmentary parts of life and the universe, he is incapable of grasping "in its entirety" the purposes that underlie it all.

Two brothers who lived in a city all their lives decided to visit the country. In the country they watched with wonder a farmer at his plowing.

"What in the world is he doing that for?" they thought. The farmer turns up the earth. Why would someone take a smooth field covered with nice green grass and dig it up? Later they saw the farmer sowing grains of wheat. "That man is an idiot. He takes good wheat and throws it into the dirt."

One brother decided to return to the city. "I don't like the country. Only queer people live here." The older brother remained and witnessed the change that gradually took place. The plowed field began to sprout and blossom even more beautifully than before. This change fascinated him so much that he wrote to his brother. He related to him the wonderful change and asked him to come back.

The brother came back and was equally amazed as the

sprouts grew into golden heads of wheat. They began to appreciate the original purpose of the farmer's work. However, when the wheat became ripe, the farmer took his scythe and began cutting it down. At this point the younger brother became impatient and said, "The farmer is crazy. Why does he take all the fine wheat and cut it down with his own hands? I am going back to the city."

The older brother remained in the country. He saw the farmer gather the wheat into his granary, separating the grain from the chaff. Only then did he realize that the farmer had harvested a hundred fold of the seed that he had originally sown. Now he understood the logic which he and his brother did not accept in the beginning.

—Dubno Maggid

12. *I realized that there is nothing better for them than to be happy and to do good in their lifetime.*

To be happy and to do good.

Rabbi Beroka frequently went to a market place at Be-Lopat where Elijah the prophet appeared to him. Once he asked the prophet Elijah, "Is there anyone in this market who has a share in the world to come?" He replied, "No."

Just then he caught sight of a man wearing black shoes and he exclaimed, "This man has a share in the world to come." Rabbi Beroka ran after him and asked him, "What is your occupation?" and the man replied that he would tell him tomorrow.

Next day Rabbi Beroka met the man and asked again, "What is your occupation?" He replied, "I am a jailer. I risk my life to establish morality there and to be kind to the prisoners." While they were speaking two men passed by and Elijah remarked, "These two have a share in the world to come."

Rabbi Beroka then approached them and asked them, "What is your occupation?" They replied, "We are jesters.

When we see people dejected and depressed, we cheer them up. Furthermore, when we see two people quarrelling, we strive hard to make peace between them."

—Talmud, Taanith p. 22a

13. *Indeed any man who eats and drinks and finds satisfaction in his occupation, that is a gift of God.*

Finds satisfaction in his occupation.

The Rabbi of Lublin said that Rabbi Isaac Luria had two chief merits. One—he explained the mysteries of the book of the Zohar. The second—that he considered rejoicing foremost in the service of God. For that reason he earned sufficient merit to see Elijah the Prophet.

Then he added, "I envy Chassidim because they possess cheerful dispositions. That makes them enjoy this world and marks them for a share in the world to come."

—Zohs Zichoron

14. *I realized that whatever God ordains shall be forever; nothing can be added to it and from it nothing can be subtracted. God has done this, that man may revere Him.*

Once again he bases his thought on the assertion that God's laws are enduring. For that reason he teaches man to accept rather than try to alter the course of life.

There was a pipe in the Sanctuary which was smooth and thin, made of reeds from the days of Moses, and its sound was pleasant. The king ordered it overlayed with gold, and its sound was no longer pleasant. Then its overlay was removed and its sound was pleasant again as before.

There was a cymbal in the Sanctuary from the days of Moses, made of bronze and its sound was pleasant. It became damaged. The sages sent for craftsmen in Alexandria of Egypt and they repaired it, but its sound was not pleasant any more. Then they removed the improvement and its sound became as pleasant as before.

The pool of Shiloah gushed forth through an opening the size of a coin. The king commanded that it be widened so that its waters would be increased but the waters diminished. Then it was narrowed again, whereupon it had its original flow. This proves the truth: "Let not the wise man boast of his wisdom, neither let the mighty man boast of his might." (Jeremiah 9:22)

—Talmud, Arachin p. 10a

15. *Whatever is has been long ago and what is to be has been long ago; God will seek the pursued.*

The teaching in this sentence is paradoxical. It begins by asserting that all is pre-ordained. Nevertheless, man has choice and free will. Because of this the persecutor will be punished and the persecuted will be favored.

God demands from the persecutors the blood of the persecuted. Abel was persecuted by Cain but God chose Abel. (Genesis 4:4) Abraham was persecuted by Nimrod but God chose Abraham. (Nehemiah 9:17) Isaac was persecuted by the Philistines but God chose Isaac. (Genesis 26:28)

Jacob was persecuted by Esau but God chose Jacob. (Psalm 135:4) Moses was persecuted by Pharoah but God chose Moses. (Psalm 106:23) David was persecuted by Saul but God chose David. (Psalm 78:70) Israel was persecuted by the peoples of the world but God chose Israel. (Deuteronomy 14:2)

It is the same with the sacrifices. God said: "The ox is persecuted by the lion, the goat by the leopard, the lamb by the wolf. Do not offer sacrifices to me of the persecutors, but rather of those persecuted."

—Midrash Rabbah, Ecclesiastes III

16. *Furthermore, I observed under the sun that in the place of justice there was iniquity and in the place of equity there was wickedness.*

In the place of justice there was iniquity.

There was a severe epidemic among the animals. The lion, tiger, bear, camel and fox met to discuss what to do in this crisis.

The fox said, "Never before have we been punished like this. Someone in the animal kingdom has committed a grave crime. I propose that we call a world council of animals and each animal confess his sins. From the confession we will see who is to be blamed for our sufferings and deal with him accordingly."

All beasts of prey confessed their sins, and their excuses for killing and devouring human beings day and night were accepted. Finally a little sheep confessed that after a hard day's work for the hunter, he didn't have enough food. He noticed the hunter's overshoes contained some hay and he ate some hay from those boots.

"Aha!" roared the lion. "You are the great sinner. You have abused and betrayed your master's confidence. The pieces of hay you stole from your master might have caused him to catch a cold." The entire world council of animals voted to condemn the sheep to death.

—Niflo'oth Rabbi Bunam

17. *I reflected in my heart, "God will judge the innocent and the guilty, for there is a time for every experience and every act—there."*

For there is a time for every experience and every act— there. The Rabbis understand the word "there" to refer to the world to come.

Those who are born are destined to die; those who are dead are to be brought to life again; and the living to be judged.

It is for them to know, proclaim and be sure that he is God. He is the Maker, He the Creator, He the Discerner, He the Judge, He the Witness, He the Complainant; it is He who will judge.

Blessed be He in whose presence there is no unrighteousness, nor forgetting, nor partiality, nor taking of bribes. Know that all is according to reckoning and let not your imagination assure you that the grave is a place of refuge for you. Against your will you were formed and against your will you were born; against your will you shall die, and against your will you shall have to give a strict account before the supreme King of kings, the Holy One, blessed be He.

—Ethics of the Fathers 4:29

18. *I reflected with regard to men that God might make it clear to them so that they may see that by themselves they are but beasts.*

That by themselves they are but beasts

A merchant hired a coachman, his horse and wagon to take him from his village to the city. The merchant fell asleep because he was tired and the coachman fell asleep because he had eaten a heavy meal, and drank a bit.

The horse went straight on the main road until he sighted some sweet smelling grass. He turned off on a narrow side road. The coach turned over and fell into a ditch, and the merchant was thrown out of the vehicle and was injured. The merchant began shouting at the coachman, "Didn't you watch where you were going?"

"My horse is well trained and very smart," the coachman said. "It never occurred to me that he would leave the main road."

This angered the merchant, "You fool, what do you mean, you trusted the horse. Your horse may be the smartest but he is still a horse. When he smelled the grass on the

85

side road he could not resist his desire and turned away from the main road."

—Chofetz Chaim on Ethics of the Fathers

19. *For that which happens to man happens to the beast; the same fate befalls them; as one dies, so does the other; the same breath is in all of them; and man has no advantage over the beast, for all is vanity.*

Man and beast suffer the same end—death. No wonder there are sceptics who hold both on the same level.

Rabbi Chezkiah and Rabbi Yossi were walking together. Rabbi Yossi said, "I see from your face that some thought is troubling you." He replied, "I am pondering the verse: 'For that which happens to man happens to the beast.' This wise saying of Solomon troubles me, because it seems to give an opening to unbelievers." "That is so," came the reply.

At that moment a man came up to them and asked for water as he was thirsty and weary from the heat of the sun.

"Have you studied Torah?" they asked the man. He answered, "Instead of talking with you, I can go up that hill and find water there to drink." Chastened, Rabbi Yossi took out a flask and gave it to him. When he had drunk, they said, "Now we will go up with you for more water."

So they all went up to the rock hill and found there a trickling stream from which they filled a bottle. Then the man said, "You asked me if I had studied Torah. I have done so through my son. From him I gained some knowledge of Torah." Rabbi Chezkiah said to him, "If it is through your son, well and good, but, then, I see, for the solution of our problem we shall have to look somewhere else."

The man said, "Let me hear it, since sometimes in the beggar's wallet one finds a pearl."

Then they quoted to him the verse of Ecclesiastes. He said to them, "How are you different from all other men who also don't know. This is the way in which Solomon meant this verse. He was not saying this in his own name, he was repeating what is said by the world of fools that, 'That which happens to man happens to the beast.' That is to say, that this world is a sport of a chance and there is no providence."

"Solomon calls these fools 'cattle' in the preceding verse: 'That they may see that they themselves are as beasts.' What did Solomon answer them? 'Who knows the spirit of man that ascends upward and the spirit of the beast that descends downward to the earth?' (Ecclesiastes 3:21)

"Who of these fools who know not of the honor of the Supreme King knows that the spirit of man goes upward to an eternal and holy place to be nourished by the supreme brightness of the Holy King and to be included, "in the bond of eternal life.' The spirit of the beast goes downward. Concerning man, it is written, 'In the image of God He made them.' "

Rabbi Chezkiah and Rabbi Yossi kissed this man on the head saying, "All this you knew and we were not aware. Blessed be the hour in which we met you."

—Zohar, Bamidbar Shlach

20. *All go to one place, all are from the dust and all return to dust.*

All are from the dust and all return to dust.

In order to create Adam God gathered dust from all corners of the earth. The dust to form Adam was of various colors: red, white, black, and green. The reason why the dust was taken from all corners of the earth is that if a man from the east should happen to die in the west, or a man from the west in the east, the earth should not refuse to receive the dead and tell him to go from where he was taken.

Wherever a man chances to die and wherever he is buried, there will he return to the earth from which he came.

—Yalkut Shimoni 1:13

All go to one place.

Rabbi Meir was teaching at the Synagogue the entire Sabbath afternoon. Meanwhile in his home, his two sons died. Beruria, the scholarly mother of these children covered their bodies with a white sheet.

When the Rabbi returned he asked his wife about the boys and she answered that they had gone to the House of Study. She gave her husband a goblet of wine to perform the Havdala service marking the conclusion of the Sabbath, and then served him his evening meal. When he had finished his meal and said grace his wife said: "I have a question to ask you."

"Ask it please," he replied. "Some time ago" she continued, "a man entrusted several precious jewels to me. Now he came to reclaim them. Should I return them or not?"

The Rabbi answered, "How can anyone hesitate to return something that belongs to its owner?" "I know" she said, "but I thought it wise to do so only with your consent."

She then took him to the room and approaching the bed she removed the sheet and he saw his two sons dead.

Rabbi Meir cried and lamented bitterly, "My sons, my sons." Then she said to him, "Did you not teach me that we must restore to the owner that which he entrusted to our care?" The Lord gave, The Lord has taken away, blessed be the name of the Lord.

—Midrash Shmuel 31

21. *Who knows the spirit of man that ascends upward and the spirit of the beast that descends downward to the earth.*

In this sentence the Hebrew syntax contains a definite article before the words "ascends" and "descends."— Prof. M. D. Kassuto. It is wrong to translate this sentence in an interrogative form. It is not "Who knows whether the spirit of man ascends and the spirit of the beast descends." The preferred translation is our text. The author's own belief and the response to this statement is found in his acceptance of God's government in life and the universe. We see this in Chapter 11:9 "But know, for all this God will bring you to account," and in Chapter 12:14 "For every deed, good or bad, even those hidden, God will bring you to judgment."

The creatures of heaven were created in His image and His likeness and do not reproduce. The animal creatures of earth reproduce but were not created in His image and likeness. Then God said: "I will form a new creature (man) that will combine both qualities. I shall create him in My Image and Likeness like the creatures of heaven and he will reproduce like the creatures of earth."

Rabbi Tarfon added: "God said, 'If I will create man only as a creature of heaven, he will live and never die. If I create man only as a creature of earth he will die and not live. Therefore I shall create him as both of heaven and earth. If he will live he will die, and if he dies he will live.' "

—Yalkut Shimoni 1:14

22. *So it appeared to me that there is nothing better for man than to be happy in his activities for that is his lot, for who can cause him to see what will be after him?*

Who can bring him to see what will be after him. The final sentence in this chapter is a fair conclusion for all men whether they be sceptic, agnostic, or the faithful. Let every man exercise his privilege of enjoying life. No one alive can foresee what will be after him.

For who will bring King David back to life to see what Solomon did? (He built the Temple and enlarged the kingdom!)

Who will bring King Solomon back to see what happened because of what his son Reheboam did? (He caused the ancient Kingdom to be divided into two kingdoms, Israel and Judah.)

—Midrash Rabbah, Ecclesiastes 3:22

CHAPTER FOUR

1. *I reconsidered all the oppressions practiced under the sun; and there were the tears of the oppressed and they had none to comfort them. In the hands of their oppressors was power, but they had none to comfort them.*

> In this chapter the author considers aspects of human failings. He begins with a comment on the cruelty exerted by those in power.

A wolf was drinking at a spring on a hillside. He looked up and saw a lamb begin to drink a little lower down. "There's my supper, if only I can find some excuse to seize it!" He called to the lamb, "How dare you muddy the water from which I am drinking!"

"No, master, no," said the lamb. "If the water be muddy up there, I cannot be the cause of it for it runs down from you to me."

"Well then," said the wolf, "why did you call me bad names this time last year?"

"That cannot be, I am only six months old."

"I don't care," snarled the wolf. "If it was not you then it was your father."

Then he rushed upon the little lamb and devoured it.

—Mishlay Shu'olim

2. *I regarded as more fortunate the dead who have already died, than the living who are still alive.*

I regarded as more fortunate the dead who have already died.

There were two ocean going ships, one leaving the harbor and one entering it. As the ship sailed out of the harbor crowds came to cheer and rejoice but no one showed joy over the ship which was entering the harbor.

A wise man remarked, the reverse would be more logical. There is no reason to rejoice over a ship which is leaving because nobody knows what storms and winds it may encounter. The ship that returns in safety offers an occasion for rejoicing.

—Midrash Rabbah, Ecclesiastes 7:1

3. *But better off than either is the one who has never been, who has never seen the evil deeds done under the sun.*

Who has never seen the evil deeds done under the sun.

The sages of the school of Shammai and the sages of the school of Hillel were in dispute for two and a half years. The wise men of the school of Shammai asserted that it were better for man not to have been created.

The wise men of the school of Hillel maintained that it is better for man to have been created than not to have been created. They finally took a vote and decided that it were better for man not to have been created than to have been created. However, now that he has been created, they concluded, let him investigate his past activities (to make amends), and let him examine his future actions (to avoid doing any wrong).

—Talmud, Eruvin p. 13b

4. *I have observed that all effort and skill in work spring from man's rivalry with his neighbor. This, too, is vanity and a striving after wind.*

Man's rivalry with his neighbor.

A dog had a piece of meat which it was carrying home in its mouth. On the way he had to go on a plank lying across a running brook. As he crossed, he looked down and saw his shadow reflected in the water. Thinking it was another dog with another piece of meat, he made up his mind to have that also. So he snapped at the shadow in the water, but as he opened his mouth the piece of meat fell out. It dropped into the water and he had none.

—Mishlay Shu'olim

5. *The fool folds his hands and devours his own flesh.*

The fool folds his hands.

Solomon said seven things about a sluggard, but what Moses said has more meaning than all of them.

Solomon: People say to the sluggard, "Your teacher is in the city, go and learn Torah from him." The lazy man answers, "I fear the lion on the highway." People say to him: "Your teacher is in this neighborhood. Get up and go to him." And he replies, "I fear lest there be a lion in the streets." They say to him, "But he lives near your house," and he replies: "The lion is outside."

They say to him: "He is in the very house." He answers: "If I go and the door (of the teacher's room) is locked, I will have to return."

They say to him, "It is open."

Finally when the sluggard does not know what further excuses to give he says to them: "Be the door opened or closed I want to sleep a little longer." When he gets up from his sleep in the morning and food is placed before him he is too lazy to put it into his mouth.

The seventh thought of Solomon: "The sluggard will not plow when the winter sets in." (Proverbs 20:14)

Moses said: "But the word is very near unto you, in your mouth and in your heart that you may do it." (Deuteronomy 30:14)

—Midrash Rabbah, Deuteronomy 8:7

6. *Better a handful with ease than two handfuls with toil and striving after wind.*

Better a handful with ease.

Better is one who gives charity to only a small extent from his own than one who robs and oppresses and gives much charity from what belongs to others. A folk-saying declares: "She prostitutes herself for apples and distributes them among the sick." A striving after wind is his striving to be called a philanthropist.

Better is he who possesses ten gold pieces with which he does business and maintains himself than he who takes money from others which he loses and causes to vanish. A proverb declares, "Not enough that he loses his own but he loses also what belongs to others, both what is his and what is not his." A striving after wind is his striving to be called a businessman.

Better is he who leases one garden and eats its fruits than he who leases many gardens and neglects them. A proverb declares, "Who leases one garden eats birds, who leases gardens will be eaten by birds." A striving after wind is his striving to be called a land owner.

—Midrash Rabbah, Ecclesiastes 4:6

7. *Again I observed an absurdity under the sun.*

An absurdity under the sun.

Alexander of Macedonia travelled to a very distant land called Katzio. Alexander sent a message to the King of Katzio to come and see him. The local king arranged a banquet to receive this great world conqueror. All was of gold. He had all food, bread, vegetables and meat formed out of gold. All was served on dishes of gold on a golden table.

Alexander sat down and admired it all. Then he attempted to eat, but could not eat the golden food. "Is that how you receive me?" Alexander said in anger. "Forgive us," said the host. "We served you food made of gold for plain food you have at home and you need not travel to the end of the earth for that."

—Midrash Rabbah, Genesis 33

8. *There is a lone man, with no companion, who has neither son nor brother; but there is no end to all his toil, nor is his eye ever satisfied with riches. "For whom am I toiling and depriving myself of pleasure?" This, too, is futility and a miserable task.*

There is a lone man.

One day a very stingy man came to see a Rabbi. This man was not only the richest man in the country, but also the greatest miser. The Rabbi took him by the hand and led him to the window looking out on the street. "What do you see?" asked the Rabbi. "I see people," answered the rich man. Then the Rabbi led the man to a mirror. "What do you see now?" "Now I see myself," the man replied.

Then the Rabbi said: "The window is made of glass and the mirror is made of glass. The only difference is that the glass of the mirror has a veneer of silver on it. When you look through plain glass you see people. No sooner do you cover it with silver when you stop seeing others and see only yourself."

—Oral Tradition

9. *Two are better than one, because they have a better reward for their labor.*

Two are better than one.

When Rabbi Meir saw a man go on the road alone, he would cry out to him, "Go in peace, O master of death," because by going alone he placed himself in danger.

When he saw two going together, he used to cry out to them, "Peace be with you, O masters of strife," because two together are likely to quarrel.

When he saw three going together, he used to say to them, "Peace be with you, O masters of peace," because when there are three, even if two quarrel the third can reconcile them.

—Midrash Rabbah, Ecclesiastes 4:9

An aged father, before he died, wanted to leave the unmistakable message that in unity there is strength. He feared lest his sons would quarrel and lose the stability of their family relationship.

He called all his sons together and asked each one in turn to break some branches of a tree tied up in a bundle. No one could. Then he untied the bundle and gave each one a single branch and each one easily broke the twigs. "This is my lesson and my instruction to all my sons," said the father. "If you will be alone, you will easily be broken, but united you will have the strength to overcome any difficulty."

—Adapted from Yalkut Amos 549

10. *For if they fall one will lift up his companion, but woe to him who is alone and falls with no one to lift him.*

One will lift up his companion.

A lonely traveller was crossing mountain heights of untrodden snow. He struggled bravely against fatigue and the feeling of sleep. At this crisis he stumbled against a heap which was lying across his path. He found it to be a human body half buried in the snow.

The next moment he held the frozen man in his arms, rubbing and massaging his limbs. The effort to restore another to life brought back to him warmth and energy and was the means of saving them both.

—Chief Rabbi Dr. Hertz of Great Britain

11. *Also, if two huddle together they keep warm, but how can one alone be warm?*

If two huddle together

After a long period of illness, a sick man finally called a physician. The doctor examined him and said, "My friend you and I and your disease are three. If you will cooperate with me the two of us will be able to ovecome your illness which is only one. If, however, you should not cooperate with me, but hold on to your disease, I, being alone, will not be able to overcome both of you."

—Bar Hebraeus

12. *If one should attack, two can stand up against him and "a threefold cord is not easily broken."*

Two can stand up against him.

The matter can be likened to two dogs who were always angry at each other. Once a wolf attacked one of them. Then the other said, "If I don't help him the wolf will kill him today and kill me tomorrow." So both went together and killed the wolf.

—Talmud, Sanhedrin p. 105a

13. *Better a poor but wise youth, than an old but fool-ish king who no longer knows to heed a warning.*

History is full of instances such as described in this verse. There are always rulers who refuse to give up power, even though they are no longer able to rule. What is worse, they do not learn from past experience.

A hunter once caught a bird. The bird asked the hunter to set him free and he would teach him three wise rules. The rules were: Never regret that which is past, never believe the unbelievable, never reach for the unattainable.

The hunter let the bird go free and it flew to the top of the highest tree nearby. The bird thanked the hunter and told him, "I have within me a pearl worth a million dollars."

Regretful of his act, the hunter jumped up and began to climb up the tree but fell and broke his neck.

The bird mocked him and said, "You have not learned anything from my teaching. I am free, now why regret the past? I am so small how could I have within me such a huge pearl? I warned you not to reach for the unattainable, yet you tried to reach the top of this tree.

—Exempla of Rabbis, Gaster

14. *For one may come out of prison to govern, while the other even in his royalty becomes poor.*

This statement aptly applies to Joseph as related in the Book of Genesis. Often in history we see a wise youth suffering every disadvantage rise to rule over one born to royalty.

Thereupon Pharaoh sent for Joseph, and he was rushed from the dungeon. He had his hair cut and changed his clothes, and he appeared before Pharaoh.

—Genesis 41:14-15

So Pharaoh said to Joseph, "Since God has made all this known to you, there is none so discerning and wise as you. You shall be in charge of my palace, and by your command shall all my people be directed; only with respect to the throne shall I be superior to you."

Pharaoh further said to Joseph, "See, I put you in charge of the whole land of Egypt." And removing his signet ring from his hand, Pharaoh put it on Joseph's hand; and he had him dressed in robes of fine linen, and put a gold chain about his neck. He had him ride in the chariot of his second-in-command, and they cried before him, "Abrek!"

Thus he put him in charge of the whole land of Egypt. Pharaoh said to Joseph, "I am Pharaoh; yet without your consent no one shall lift up hand or foot in all the land of Egypt." Pharaoh then called Joseph's name Zaphenath-paneah and married him to Asenath, daughter of Poti-phera, priest of On. Thus Joseph emerged in charge of the land of Egypt.

—Genesis 41:39-45

15. *I have seen all the people who walk under the sun with the youthful successor who was to replace him.*

With the youthful successor. This too has been repeated in history. The old king is soon forgotten and "all the people flock to acclaim the new hero."

Jeroboam, the son Nebat, an Ephraimite of Zeredah, a servant of Solomon, also lifted up his hand against the king. Solomon therefore sought to kill Jeroboam, but Jeroboam arose and fled to Egypt to Shishak, king of Egypt, and was in Egypt till the death of Solomon.

—I Kings 11:26, 40

Now as soon as all Israel heard that Jeroboam had returned they sent and called him to the assembly and made him king over all Israel. None remained loyal to the house of David except the tribe of Judah alone.

—I Kings 12:20

16. *There was no end to all the people, to all whose leader he was; nevertheless later generations will not be happy with him. Surely, this too is vanity and a striving after wind.*

Now Koheleth concludes with another historical fact. The new leader, so popular among the people of his day, will not long retain his popularity.

How does a scholar appear in the eyes of an ignorant man? At first acquaintance the scholar appears to him like a golden pitcher. However, on holding conversation with him, he appears like a silver pitcher. On accepting benefit from the ignoramus the scholar appears like a vessel of earthenware which once broken, cannot be repaired.

—Talmud, Sanhedrin p. 52b

17. *Guard your steps when you go to the house of God. More acceptable is obedience than the offering of a sacrifice by fools; for they do not realize that they do wrong.*

This chapter deals with the weakness of human society and of human rule. It closes with reliance on prayer to God. Worship is then connected with morality and ethics. The Talmud (Berochoth 23a) gives the following interpretation: Guard yourself against sin by obeying the words of the sages. Then be not like fools who sin and bring a sacrifice without repenting.

King Agrippa wished to offer one thousand burnt offerings in one day. He went to tell the High Priest: "Let no man beside myself offer sacrifices today!"

There came a poor man with two turtle doves in his hands. He said to the High Priest, "Sacrifice these."

The High Priest told him, "The King commanded me saying, 'Let no other man than myself offer sacrifices today.' "

Said the poor man, "My Lord High Priest, I catch four doves every day; two I offer up and with the other two I sustain myself. If you do not offer them up you cut off my means of sustenance." The High Priest took them and offered them up.

In a dream it was revealed to King Agrippa: the sacrifices of a poor man preceded yours. So he went up to the High Priest saying: "Did I not command you, 'Let no one but me offer sacrifices this day?' "

The High Priest told the King the episode of the poor man. Said the King to him, "You were right in doing as you did."

—Midrash Rabbah, Leviticus 3

CHAPTER FIVE

1. *Never be rash with your speech; never let your heart be hasty to express words before God; for God is in heaven and you are on earth; therefore let your words be few.*

The shortest prayer recorded in the Bible is that of Moses on behalf of his sister Miriam, "Please, O Lord, heal her." (Numbers 12:13)

Rabbi Yossi said, "Once I travelled across the country and I came to a ruined house. It was one of the houses wrecked at the destruction of Jerusalem. I went inside and recited my prayers. When I left the house Elijah greeted me. He said to me, 'My son, why do you enter a house like this to say your prayers? You could have said your prayers while walking in the field. It is very dangerous to go into a ruined house.'

"So I replied, 'If I had said my prayers on the road, I was afraid people meeting me would confuse me.'

"Then Elijah replied, 'You should have recited a short prayer on the road.'

"From this episode I learned three lessons: One, that a person must not walk into a wrecked house. Two, that one may say his prayers while walking along the road. Three, that one who prays while on the road may say a short prayer."

—Talmud, Berochoth p. 3a

*2. As a dream comes because of many concerns, so the
fool speaks in many words.*

A dream comes with many concerns.

The Roman emperor said to Rabbi Joshua ben Chanania:
"You profess to be very clever. Tell me what shall I see in
my dream."

The Rabbi answered, "You will see the Persians take
you to do forced labor, robbing you and making you feed
unclean animals with a golden implement." The emperor
thought about it all day and at night he saw all this in his
dream.

King Shapor once said to Samuel: "You are supposed
to be very clever. Tell me what I shall see in my dream." He
answered, "You will see the Romans come and take you
captive and make you grind dates in a golden mill." He
thought about it the whole day and at night he saw this in
his dream.

—Talmud, Berochoth p. 56a

*3. When you make a vow to God do not delay fulfilling
it, for He has no pleasure in fools. Whatever you vow, fulfill.*

Whatever you vow, fulfill.

Rabbi Chanina ben Dosa saw all his neighbors taking offerings they had vowed and freewill offerings to Jerusalem. He
thought, everybody is bringing offerings to Jerusalem but
he has nothing to bring. What did he do? He went outside
of his city and saw there a stone which he chipped, chiseled
and polished. Then he said, "Behold, I take it upon myself
to convey it to Jerusalem."

He looked to hire workmen and five men happened to
come his way. He asked them, "Will you carry up this
stone for me to Jerusalem?" They answered, "Give us five
coins and we will carry it up to Jerusalem." He would have

given them the money but he had none with him at the time. They left him.

Later, five angels appeared to him in the likeness of men. Rabbi Chanina asked them, "Will you carry up this stone for me?" They answered, "Give us five coins and we will carry up your stone for you to Jerusalem, but on condition that you also help."

He placed his hand and fingers with theirs and they found themselves standing in Jerusalem. The Rabbi wanted to pay them but he could not find them.

—Midrash Rabbah, Ecclesiastes 1:1

4. *It is better not to vow, than to vow and not fulfill.*

It is better not to vow.

Be sure that if you make a vow to fulfill that vow. Reflect on Jonah. He made a vow and did not fufill it. What happened to him? He was lowered to the depth of the sea. When he was thrown into the sea he reminded himself that he once made a vow. He prayed to God and he said: "Lord of the Universe, I know that I made a vow and did not perform it. Now if I am saved from this trouble I will carry out my promise to you."

Jonah said: "Out of my trouble I called unto the Lord and He answered me. (Jonah 2:2) "I will sacrifice to you with the voice of thanksgiving. What I have vowed, I will pay." (Jonah 2:9)

—Yalkut Shimoni, Matos 784

5. *Let not your mouth cause guilt to your body and plead not before the messenger, "it was a mistake." Why should God be angry at your speech and destroy what you have accomplished.*

In the event you make a pledge to a sacred cause, you dishonor God by breaking your promise. Then a penalty is inevitable.

Jephthah made a vow to the Lord saying, "If you will but deliver the Ammonites into my power, whosoever comes out of the door of my house to meet me, when I return in peace from the Ammonites, shall be the Lord's; I will offer him up as a burnt-offering."

Then Jephthah crossed over to the Ammonites, to fight against them and the Lord delivered them into his power. He smote them with a very great slaughter from Aroer as far as the vicinity of Minnith, through twenty cities and as far as Abel-cheramin. And the Ammonites were brought into subjection to the Israelites.

Then Jephthah came home to Mizpah, and there his daughter came out to meet him with tambourines and dancing! She was his only child, besides her he had neither son nor daughter. Upon seeing her, he tore his clothes, and said, "Alas, my daughter, you have stricken me low! You have brought calamity on me! For I made a vow to the Lord, and I cannot repudiate it."

"My father," she said to him, "since you have made a vow to the Lord, do to me as you declared, now that the Lord has taken vengeance for you on your enemies, the Ammonites. But let this privilege be granted me." She said to her father, "Spare me for two months, that I may go and roam at large on the mountains, and bewail my maidenhood, I and my companions."

"Go," he said.

And he sent her away for two months, and she and her companions went to bewail her maidenhood on the mountains. Then, at the end of two months she returned to her father, who did to her what he had vowed, and she had not known a man.

—Judges 11:30-40

Jephthah made a vow, "Whosoever comes out of the door of my house to meet me when I return in peace from the Ammonites shall be the Lord's: I will offer him up as a burnt offering."

At that time God was displeased. Suppose a dog, swine or a camel were first to meet him, would he sacrifice a dog, swine or camel to me? It was his daughter who came to meet him. Why? To teach the world that those who make vows should be aware of the consequence of making vows. Vows are never to be made compulsively.

—Midrash Tanchuma, Bechukosay 5

6. *Multitudes of dreams and vanities result in a multitude of words, but you fear God.*

But you fear God.

When Rabbi Yochanan ben Zakkai was ill his disciples came to visit him. As soon as he saw them he began to weep. His disciples said to him, "Lamp of Israel, great and honored Master, why do you weep?"

He replied: "If I were taken before a human king who is here today and gone tomorrow, whose wrath, if he is angry with me, does not last forever; who, if he imprisons me, does not imprison me forever, and if he should put me to death does not put me to everlasting death, and whom I can appease with words and bribe with money, even so I would weep. Now that I am taken before the Supreme King of Kings, the Holy One Blessed be He, who lives and rules forever should I not cry?

"This is not all. There are two ways before me, one leading to Paradise and the other to Gehinom and I do not know which way they are going to lead me."

The disciples said to him, "Master, bless us."

The Rabbi replied, "May it be (God's) will that you should fear God as much as you fear men."

107

The disciples said, "Is that all?" (Should not fear of God be more than that of man?)

The Rabbi answered, "If only you do that. You see that when a man commits a sin he says, 'I hope no man will see me.' "

—Talmud, Berochoth p. 28b

7. *If you see the exploitation of the poor and the perversion of justice and righteousness in the state, do not be perplexed at the situation, for there is an official watching an official and over them are higher officials.*

If you see the exploitation of the poor

A lion went hunting together with the fox, jackal, and wolf. They hunted until they caught a deer and killed it. Then came the question how to divide the spoils.

"Quarter me this deer," said the lion. The other animals skinned it and cut it into four parts. Then the lion said, "The first quarter is for me in my capacity as king of the beasts; the second is mine as arbiter; the third comes to me for my share in the hunting; and as for the fourth, I would like to see who would dare to take it away from me."

—Mishlay Shu'olim

8. *The advantage of land is above all else, even the king is devoted to the soil.*

The advantage of land.

Even if a king rules from one end of the earth to the other, he is enslaved to the field. For if the soil produces he has achieved, but if the soil is unproductive he can accomplish nothing.

Whoever is greedy and covets money but has no land, what benefit does he derive? (This indicates the enduring value of land as opposed to the fleeting nature of money.)

The prophet Ezekiel (27:29) says: "All the oarsmen and sailors and all the pilots of the sea shall come down from their ships, they shall stand upon the land."

The Rabbis ask, "Don't we know when they come ashore they now stand upon the land?" But to learn that should the ship of a man sink then if he possesses landed property, it will provide support for him. If he has no such asset there is no greater vanity than this.

—Midrash Rabbah, Ecclesiastes 5:8

9. *He who loves money is never satisfied with money and he who loves riches never has enough income; this too is vanity.*

He who loves riches never has enough income.

One day a farmer going to the nest of his goose found there an egg, yellow and glittering. He picked it up. It was heavy as lead and he was going to discard it. On second thought he took it to the house. The more he looked at the egg the more it seemed worth the effort of taking it to town to inquire what it is. To his delight he was told that it is an egg of gold. Every morning he found just such a golden egg.

Soon he became very rich by selling his golden eggs. As he grew richer, he grew more greedy. He thought of a plan to get all the gold the goose could give. He killed the goose and opened it up to find it empty.

—Harvard Classics

10. *When prosperity increases, they increase who consume it; then of what value is it to its owner except feasting his eyes.*

Except feasting his eyes.

There was a miser who used to hide his jewelry and his

109

money at the foot of a tree in his garden. Every week he used to go, dig it up and gloat over his possessions.

A robber who discovered this went and dug it all up and took the entire fortune away. Next time the miser came to gloat over his money he found nothing but the empty hole. He began lamenting and crying so loudly that all his neighbors came around. He told the neighbors about his regular weekly visits to see his gold and now it is all gone.

"Did you ever take any of it out?" he was asked.

"No, I only came to look at it."

—Harvard Classics

11. *Sweet is the sleep of the laborer whether he eat little or much, but the over-abundance of the rich man will not let him sleep.*

Sweet is the sleep of the laborer.

Rabbi Yehudah the Prince, after a bath, dressed and sat down to receive the people waiting to see him. The servant mixed a drink of wine and water for the Rabbi. Being busy with the people, the Rabbi had no chance to take it from him. Waiting to serve the Rabbi the servant became drowsy and fell asleep.

The Rabbi looked in the direction of his servant and seeing that he is sleeping exclaimed, "Solomon correctly said, 'Sweet is the sleep of the laborer.' As for me, I am too busy attending to the needs of the people."

—Midrash Rabbah, Ecclesiastes 5:11

12. *There is a painful evil which I have seen under the sun; wealth hoarded by its owner to his own hurt.*

Wealth hoarded by its owner to his own hurt.

A scheming fellow came to his rich neighbor to borrow a silver spoon. Several days later the borrower returned the spoon and with it a little silver spoon. "I lent you only one spoon." "Your spoon," replied the borrower, "gave birth to this little spoon. So mother and child belong to you."

Several weeks later the man came to his neighbor and asked him to lend him a large silver goblet. The avaricious neighbor was happy to give him a goblet. The borrower returned with the goblet and a little goblet. "Your goblet gave birth to this little goblet and I brought both of them to you."

Some time passed and this man approached his neighbor and asked that he lend him a gold watch. Thinking that his neighbor would return his watch with a little watch he gladly gave the gold watch.

The borrower failed to return with the watch. The rich man became impatient and went to see his neighbor. "What about my watch," he asked. The borrower gave a deep sigh, "I regret to tell you that your watch is dead!"

"Dead, what do you mean dead. How can a watch die?"

The scheming man answered, "If spoons and goblets can reproduce, then a watch can die."

—Dubno Maggid

13. *His wealth is lost through a bad investment and then a son is born to him and he has nothing left in his hand.*

He has nothing left in his hand.

Rabbi Chiyah said to his wife: "When a poor man comes, be quick to offer him bread so that others may be quick to offer it to your children."

"You appear to curse them," she exclaimed.

The Rabbi replied, "Money is a wheel that revolves in the world.

"There is a verse that the School of Rabbi Yishmael interpreted: 'And he shall show you mercy and have compassion upon you and multiply you.' He who is merciful to others, mercy is shown to him by Heaven, while he who is not merciful to others, mercy is not shown to him by Heaven."

—Talmud, Sabbath p. 151b

14. *As he came from his mother's womb, naked shall he return, going as he came; and for his toil he has nothing to take with him.*

> The psalmist (Psalm 49) says: "Fear not when man grows rich, when the splendor of his house increases, for he will take nothing with him when he dies; his wealth will not follow him below."

As a man enters the world so he departs. He enters with a vocal sound and leaves the world with a vocal sound. He enters the world with weeping and he departs with weeping. He enters the world in love and takes leave of the world in love. He enters the world with a sigh and departs with a sigh. He enters the world devoid of knowledge and departs devoid of knowledge. Rabbi Meir taught: When a person enters the world his hands are clenched as if he would indicate the whole world is mine. I shall acquire it! When he departs from the world his hands are spread open as if to proclaim, "I have taken nothing from the world."

—Midrash Rabbah, Ecclesiastes 5:14

15. *And this, too, is a painful evil, exactly as he came he must depart; so what profit has he who toils for the wind?*

Exactly as he came he must depart.

A king distributed gifts to his officers and servants. One officer noticed that the gift he received was not of silver but an imitation.

This officer said to the king "I cannot accept your gift because it would seem as if you are paying me for my services. I am, as you know, serving you without any compensation. Therefore I would like you in turn to accept one silver coin from me." The king agreed. When the king examined the coin he said, "This coin is counterfeit." The officer responded, "Yes, it is like your gift to me."

—Dubno Maggid

16. *All his days he even eats in the dark and he has much grief, illness and anger.*

And he has much grief, illness and anger.

To have a "generous eye" is to be content with one's portion and delight in what God has given him. If what he has is little, let him regard it as though it were plentiful.

To have a "grudging eye" is to acquire possessions and riches and honor and regard them all as though they were only a little. Such a man pursues the vanities of the world in order to satisfy his appetite for more and more. All his days are filled with pain, anguish, sickness, and wrath.

—Joseph ben Judah ibn Aknin

17. *Behold, this is what I have observed: it is good and proper to eat and drink and to enjoy pleasure with all the gains one has earned under the sun, during the span of life which God has allotted to one, for that is one's lot.*

As a result of his observations of the perversion of justice and the miser's miserable existence, the author reccommends not asceticism, but the enjoyment of life in a moral setting.

Raba asked Rafram ben Papa: "Tell me some of the good deeds Rabbi Huna performed."

He answered, "I do not remember him in his youth, but I remember him in his old age. Following stormy weather they used to drive him around in a golden carriage. He would survey every part of the city and he would order any wall that was unsafe to be demolished. If the owner was in a position to do it he had to rebuild it himself. If not, then Rabbi Huna would rebuild it at his own expense.

"Every Friday, late afternoon, Habbi Huna would send a messenger to the market and buy up all the vegetables that the gardners had left over and have them thrown into the river (that the merchants be free to go home and prepare for the Sabbath).

"When a new medicine was discovered he would proclaim that whoever needs it may come and get it to save his life. When he had a meal he would open the door wide and declare that 'whoever is in need, let him come and eat.' "

—Talmud, Taanith p. 20b

18. *Furthermore, every man to whom God has given wealth, possessions and the power to enjoy it, to take his portion and be happy in his work, this is a gift of God.*

The power to enjoy it.

It happened that King Munbaz had distributed his treasures and the treasures of his fathers in years of scarcity. His brothers and his father's household complained to him. They said to him, "Your father saved and added savings to the treasures of his father and you are squandering them."

The king replied, "My fathers stored up below and I store up in heaven. My fathers stored up in a place where the treasure can be tampered with by human hands and I store in a place where it cannot be tampered with by human hands. My fathers stored something which yielded no fruit but I have stored something which does yield fruit. My fathers saved money in their treasury, but I have saved souls in my treasury. My fathers saved for others and I saved for myself. My fathers gathered for this world, but I have gathered for the world to come."

—Talmud, Baba Bathra p. 11a

114

19. *For let him remember that the days of his life are not many; that God has decreed the joy of his heart.*

Remember that the days of his life are not many.

Mar, son of Rabina made a wedding feast for his son. He saw his guests growing merry so he brought an expensive crystal and broke it before them and they became serious.

Rabbi Ashi made a wedding feast for his son. He saw the Rabbis were getting very merry. He then brought a cup of white crystal and broke it before them and they became serious.

The Rabbis said to Rabbi Hamuna Zuta at the wedding of Mar, the son of Rabina, "Please sing something for us."

He replied, "Alas, for us that we have to die. Alas for us that we have to die."

They asked him, "What shall be our response."

He said to them, "Where is the Torah and where is the mitzvah (good deed) that will shield us?"

—Talmud, Berochoth p. 30b

CHAPTER SIX

1. *There is an evil which I observed under the sun and it is prevalent among men.*

There is an evil which I observed.

Rabbi Samuel ben Ammi said this refers to devices of cheats who dilute wine with water; oil with a poppy juice; honey with a wild strawberry juice. They use a weight-beam which is longer on one side than the other to give false measure.

Rabbi Yochanan ben Zakkai remarked concerning this, "it pains me to say it, it pains me if I don't say it. If I tell of this there is the danger that cheats will learn what to do. If I don't reveal it, the cheats may believe that the Sages are unacquainted with their actions."

—Midrash Rabbah, Ecclesiastes 6:1

2. *A man to whom God grants wealth, possessions and position so that he lacks nothing he may desire, but God has not given him power to enjoy it, for some stranger will consume it. This is vanity and an evil affliction.*

But God has not given him power to enjoy it.

The Preacher of Dubno came to solicit a contribution of charity from a miser. He was a very wealthy and powerful man, but he would not give any charity. The miser bluntly refused to give. The Rabbi then got up to leave and he said to the miser, "You are destined for a share in the world to come."

The rich man, puzzled and perplexed, said, "When I refuse a contribution I never receive such a blessing. I would like to know why this compliment."

"Let me tell you a story," replied the Rabbi.

"Once there was a very rich man, a notorious miser who never gave anything to charity. Before his death he made a will that all his money, his gold, his silver and diamonds were to be buried with him in his coffin. When he passed away he came before the Court in Heaven. In the book there was no record of charity. He was asked, 'Why is it that you kept such great wealth and never gave any charity?'

"He answered, 'I would not waste my money on idlers, liars, and cheats. If I had given my wealth in that earthly world of falsehood, it would have gone to undeserving people. I therefore decided to keep my entire fortune and bring it here to the World of Truth. I am now ready to distribute all my money for charity.'

"This was a novel defense. It took a brief session for the Heavenly Court to issue a decision. If three people would be found who have done this same thing, all would go to Paradise. The judges sought in the records and found only one. Korach, one of the richest men of all times, was swallowed up by the ground with all his possessions. This was one case of one taking all his wealth to the grave. The rich man of our story is only the second, therefore he has no rest. But now that you have followed this same path you will be three and all three will be able to gain a share in the world to come."

—Dubno Maggid, Volume I, p. 43

3. *If a man has a hundred children and lives many years, be his life ever so long, but he derives no satisfaction*

from his wealth, were he to have no burial, I declare that a stillborn child is better off than he.

If a man has a hundred children.

Every man has three friends: his family, his money and his good deeds. When he is about to pass away he calls each one and pleads, "Save me." His family answers, "No man can redeem his brother from death." (Psalm 49).

His money responds, "Wealth is of no avail on the day of wrath." (Proverbs 11:4)

But his good deeds say to him: "Before you will appear for judgment we will precede you. As it is written: 'And your righteousness shall go before you and the glory of the Lord shall be your rear guard.' " (Isaiah 58:8)

—Pirke D'Reb Eliezer XXXIV

4. *For it (the stillborn child) comes in vain and departs in darkness and its name will be shrouded in darkness.*

For it (the stillborn child) comes in vain and departs in darkness.

Why did I not die at birth, come forth from the womb and expire? Why did the knees receive me? Or why the breasts, that I should suck? For then I had lain down and been quiet, I should have slept; then were I at rest with kings and counselors of the earth, who rebuild ruins for themselves; or with nobles who had gold, who filled their houses with silver. Or like a hidden untimely birth I had not been, like infants that never saw light.

—Job 3:11-16

5. *It (the stillborn child) has neither seen nor known the sun. This has more rest than the other.*

This has more rest than the other.

119

Two men were sailing on a ship. When they reached the harbor, one of them disembarked and went into the city. There he saw much food and drink and luxury. On returning to the ship he asked his friend who remained on the ship, "Why didn't you go to the city?"

He answered, "Tell me, what did you, who went through the trouble of landing and entering the city, what did you see there?"

"I saw much food and drink and luxury," he replied.

"Did you enjoy any of it?"

"No," was the answer.

"Then," the man who stayed said, "I, who did not enter the city am much better off than you, not having landed and seen it."

—Midrash Rabbah, Ecclesiastes 6:5

6. *Even if one lives twice a thousand years and experiences no contentment, do not all go to the same place?*

Even if one lives twice a thousand years.

Rabbi Z'eira was asked by his disciples, "By what virtue have you reached such a good old age?"

The Rabbi replied, "Never in my life have I been harsh with my household. I never preceded my superiors. I never studied in unclean places, nor have I gone without tefilin and Torah. I never rejoiced in the misfortune of a fellowman and never called a man by his nickname."

—Talmud, Megillah p. 28a

7. *All a man's toil is for his mouth, and yet his appetite is never satisfied.*

All a man's toil is for his mouth.

On a severe winter night Rabbi Pinchos of Koretz sat in his study deeply involved in meditation and thought. Suddenly he heard someone knocking at the door pleading to come in. The Rabbi opened the door.

The visitor was half frozen but begged forgiveness for disturbing the Rabbi in the middle of the night. He explained that he was a merchant who covered a territory of all villages and towns in the region. He had expected to reach this city earlier, but the weather delayed his arrival. At that late hour he could not find a room in any inn. He saw a light in the Rabbi's house. He could no longer stand the snow and frost and he dared to come in and warm up.

The Rabbi offered him some food and invited him to remain overnight.

Inspired by the spiritual atmosphere in the Rabbi's house, the merchant said, "I would like to ask you a question. As you see I work hard. I travel from village to village, always on the road. I am away from my home and my family. I rarely get a night's sleep. I really don't enjoy life. As a result I don't have much of the pleasures of this world. Tell me, Rabbi, will I at least have a share in the world to come?"

The Rabbi replied, "My dear friend, I would not like to pain you or destroy your future hopes. You are in business. Do you ever get or give anything for nothing? Just consider, you work so hard day and night for the things of this world and you admit you have so little for it. How do you expect things of the world to come, for which you do nothing?"

—Nofess Tzufim

8. *For what advantage has a wise man over a fool or a poor man who knows how to face the problems of life?*

For what advantage has a wise man over a fool

A band of blind men were walking on the road. A stranger came up to one of them and said, "Here is a bagful of money. Divide it among yourselves."

But in fact he had not given them anything. As soon as he left each of the group asked the other for his share believing that the others had cheated him. Each one thought that the others were keeping the money and refusing to give him his share. They continued quarreling with one another, each one thinking that he alone was unrewarded.

—Dubno Maggid

9. *Better is what the eyes can see than the pursuit of desire, this too is vanity and a striving after wind.*

Better is what the eyes can see than the pursuit of desire.

A fisherman after fishing all day caught only a little fish. "Please let me go," cried the little fish. "I am much too small for a meal now. If you put me back into the river I shall soon grow. Then you can make a fine meal of me."

"No, my little fish," replied the fisherman. "I have you now, I may never catch you later."

—Mishlay Shu'olim

10. *Whatever happens has been ordained long ago and it is known what man is, that he cannot contend with what is mightier than he.*

Whatever happens has been ordained long ago.

Forty days before the embryo is formed a voice announces, "The daughter of this person is to be the wife of that person." Once Rabba overheard a young man praying: "May that girl be destined to be mine."

Rabba said to the young man, "Don't pray this way. If she is destined for you, you will not lose her and if she is not for you, you have challenged Providence."

Sometimes later Rabba overheard this young man praying that either he should die before her or she before him.

Rabba said to him, "Didn't I tell you not to pray in such a matter of destiny?"

—Talmud, Moed Koton p. 18b

11. *Since many possessions increase vanity, of what advantage are they to man?*

Many possessions increase vanity.

Two yeshivah students studied together. Eventually one left the yeshivah and was most successful in establishing a colossal business. The other remained in the yeshivah with his ambition to become a scholar.

One day the scholar decided to visit his wealthy friend in his business. He was impressed with the clerks, salesmen and workmen in this huge establishment. After a long wait his friend greeted him and asked to be excused. He had not a free moment. "Come and have dinner with us tonight at my home and we will talk about olden times."

In the evening the guest arrived, but the host was not home. The hostess apologized and complained that her husband worked day and night and had little time for his home and family.

Hours later the merchant, weary and hungry, arrived. At dinner the guest could not refrain from telling his host of his serene life that he would not change for all the wealth in the world. "It is true that you have amassed great wealth, but haven't you paid heavily for your success? What good is all the money if you cannot find time to enjoy it. Why, you have no time even for your home or your family."

—Dubno Maggid, Ethics of the Fathers 6:4

12. *Who knows what is good for man in his life, the numbered days of his futile existence which pass like a shadow? Who can tell a man what will happen after him under the sun?*

The numbered days of his futile existence which pass like a shadow. The chapter closes with three reasons for accepting one's lot in life. First, there is no unanimous agreement as to what constitutes the good life. Second, life is fleeting. Third, no one can predict the future with certainty.

"As a shadow" of what? If life is like the shadow of a wall, there is essence in it. If like the shadow cast by a date-palm, there is essence in it.

The Psalms of David came and explained: "His days are a shadow that passes away." (Psalm 144) Rabbi Huna said in the name of Rabbi Acha: "Life is like a bird which flies past and its shadow passes with it." Samuel said: "It (life) is like the shadow of bees in which there is no substance at all."

—Midrash Rabbah, Ecclesiastes I:2

CHAPTER SEVEN

1. *A good name is better than good oil and the day of death than the day of one's birth.*

A good name is better than good oil.

When Rabbi Yochanan on reading the book of Job used to say: "The end of man is to die and the end of cattle is to be slaughtered and all are doomed to die. Happy is he who has been reared in Torah and whose labor was in Torah; who pleased his Creator and has grown up with a good name and departed the world with a good name."

Just of such a good man, Solomon said: "A good name is better than good oil."

—Talmud, Berochoth p. 17a

A Good Name

Rabbi Yossi said, the names of people fall into four classes. Some have pleasant names and do ugly deeds. Others have unseemly names but perform fair deeds. Some have repulsive names and do repelling deeds, and there are still others who have pleasant names and do pleasant deeds. Essau and Ishmael had fair names but their deeds were not so. "Essau" means he does the will of God, but he did not. "Ishmael" means, he obeys God but he did not do so.

125

The children of the Exile of Babylon had unseemly names but their deeds were fair. They were called "Children of Bakbuk" (doubt), the Children of Hakufa (smiting) and the Children of Harhur (wrath). (Ezra 2:51) Yet they were the ones who went up and rebuilt the Holy Temple in Jerusalem.

The spies whom Moses sent out had repulsive names and their deeds were likewise. The name "Sethur" denotes destruction and the name "Godee" denotes bitterness.

The Heads of our twelve tribes had pleasant names and pleasant deeds. "Reuven," means see a son outstanding among sons, while "Shimon" indicates one who listens to the voice of his father in Heaven.

—Midrash Rabbah, Genesis Vayetze 71:4

2. *It is better to go to the house of mourning than to go to the house of feasting, because that is the end of every man, and the living will take it to heart.*

That is the end of every man.

Rabbi Eliezer was sick and Rabbi Yochanan came to visit him. He found Rabbi Eliezer lying in a dark room. Rabbi Yochanan uncovered his arm and light radiated from it and he saw that Rabbi Eliezer was crying.

"Why do you weep?" asked Rabbi Yochanan. "Is it because you did not study enough Torah? We were taught that the amount is not of much importance so long as one's intention is directed to Heaven. Are you weeping because you are poor? Not everybody has the privilege to have both wealth and wisdom. Are you weeping because of children? This is the bone of my tenth son."

Rabbi Eliezer said to him, "I am lamenting the thought that such a beautiful creature as you will have to die some day and rot in the earth."

Rabbi Yochanan replied, "On account of that you surely have reason to cry," and they both cried.

—Talmud, Berohoth p. 5b

3. *Seriousness is better than laughter, for through sadness of face the heart improves.*

Seriousness is better than laughter.

Solomon said: "If my father had been stricter with Adonijah (fourth son of King David who unsuccessfully conspired to ascend the throne of his father—I Kings 1:5), it would have done him more good than the laughter which surrounded him. If my father David had shown him a displeased countenance it might have led him to mend his ways."

It was the same with Amnon (oldest son of King David who met a tragic death on account of his lust for his half sister Tamar—II Samuel XIII). If his father David had been stricter with him it would have done him more good than the laughter which surrounded him.

—Midrash Rabbah, Ecclesiastes 7:3

4. *The heart of the wise is in the house of mourning, but the heart of fools is in the house of amusement.*

A mediaeval scholar comments that the thoughts of a wise man have a serious orientation, because he thinks of the day of death.

A sage lectured to his students, "You ought to repent one day before your death." Rabbi Eliezer was asked by his disciples: "Rabbi, does anyone know when he will die so that he can repent?" The Rabbi answered them, "Should

127

not one all the more repent today lest he die the day after. Then all his days will be lived in repentance.

—Midrash Rabbah, Ecclesiastes 9:8

5. *It is better to listen to the censure of the wise than for one to listen to the praise of fools.*

Better to listen to the censure of the wise.

Better is the curse which Achiyah pronounced upon Israel than the blessing with which Ballam the wicked, blessed them. Achiyah cursed them by compairing them to a reed. (I Kings 14:5) Israel is the reed. The reed grows by the water and its stock blossoms new shoots and its roots are many. Even though the winds of the world blow at it they can not move it from its place. The reed sways with the wind and as soon as it stops the reed resumes its upright position.

But Ballam, the wicked, blessed them by comparing them to a cedar. (Numbers 24:6) The cedar does not grow by the water, its stock does not grow new shoots and its roots are few. The cedar does not sway with the wind. If the south wind blows at it, it uproots the cedar and turns it upside down.

—Talmud, Taanith p. 20a

6. *Like the noise of thorns under a pot, so is the laughter of the fool; this too is vanity.*

Like the noise of thorns under a pot.

When all other woods are kindled their sound does not travel far, but when thorns are kindled, their sound travels far, as though to proclaim "We too are wood."

—Midrash Rabbah, Ecclesiastes 7:6

The rivers said to the Euphrates: "Why is not your sound audible?" Euphrates replied, "My deeds make me known. I don't need to shout my merits. When someone plants a plant near me it matures in thirty days. When a man sows a vegetable near me it is full grown in thirty days."

The rivers said to the Tigris: "Why is your sound audible?" The Tigris answered: "May my voice be heard that I may be seen."

They asked fruit bearing trees: "Why is your sound not audible?" "We don't need it since our fruits testify for us."

They asked the non-fruit bearing trees: "Why is your sound audible?" They answered: "We wish we could make our voice heard so that we might be seen."

—Midrash Rabbah, Genesis 16

7. *For extortion deprives a wise man of reason and a bribe corrupts the heart.*

A bribe corrupts the heart.

Rabbi Yishmoel ben Yossi had a gardener tenant who used to bring a basket of fruit as rent every Friday. On one occasion he brought it on Thursday. The Rabbi asked, "Why this change?" The gardener answered, "I have a lawsuit before you and thought at the same time I might bring the fruit to the Master."

The Rabbi did not accept the basket of fruit from him and said, "I am disqualified to act as your Judge." He then appointed two Rabbis to judge the case for him. As the Rabbi was busy with other affairs he began to think of possible arguments that might be presented in favor of his gardener tenant. "How desperate must be the plight of those who take bribes," he said to himself. "I have not taken the fruit at all, even had I taken it I would only have taken what is my own. If I am in such a state of mind, how much more those who accept bribes."

—Talmud, Kethuboth p. 105b

8. *Better is the end of a matter than its beginning. Better is patience than pride.*

Better is patience.

Birds were flying to a warm country. Among them was one rare multi-colored bird. This bird went to the top of the tallest tree and made a nest in its leaves.

When the governor of the region heard it, he sought a way to get the bird and its nest. He ordered a number of men to make a human ladder up to the top of the tree. It took a long time to build this living ladder. Those who stood nearest the ground did not know what was happening far above, lost patience, shook themselves free and everything collapsed.

—Baal Shemtov

9. *Do not quickly give way to anger, for anger rests in the bosoms of fools.*

Do not quickly give way to anger.

He who tears his garments in his anger, he who breaks his dishes in anger, and he who throws his money in anger, you may regard him as an idolator. Such are the wiles of Satan. Today he says to him, "Do this," and tomorrow he tells him, "Do that" until he tells him, "Go and serve idols," and he goes and serves them.

—Talmud, Sabbath p. 105b

A heathen smashed a marble table because a certain kind of nuts were not on it. He was so much given to material pleasure that he could not stand the lack of one dainty dish on that expensive table.

—Exempla of Rabbis 322, Gaster

10. *Do not say, "How is it that the former days were better than these?" It is not out of wisdom that you have asked about this.*

Former days were better than these?

A man was traveling through a forest. He met a wolf on the road. He escaped from this danger and told often of the experience with the wolf. Later on he met a lion. Again he escaped from the jaws of the lion. Now he told how he escaped certain death from a lion. After that a snake came near him. On escaping death from the snake he forgot altogether about the dangers he had met before. He spoke only of the escape from the snake.

—Jerusalem Talmud, Berochoth Chapter 1:6

11. *Wisdom with inheritance is good and an advantage to those who see the sun.*

Rabbi Gamliel, the son of Rabbi Yehuda the Prince, said: "Excellent is the study of Torah when it is combined with some worldly occupation for the energy taken up by both of them keeps sin out of one's mind."

—Ethics of the Fathers 2:2

Rabbi Chanina and Rabbi Cheyah were engaged in a dispute. Rabbi Chanina asked, "You argue with me? If God forbid, the Torah were forgotten in Israel, I would restore it out of my deep and extensive knowledge."

Rabbi Cheyah replied, "I have better means that the Torah shall not be forgotten in Israel. I sow flax seeds and later weave nets from the fibers. With these nets I hunt and trap deer stags. The meat, after slaughter, I feed to orphans. From the skins I make scrolls. With these scrolls I go to the cities where there are no teachers for young children. I write on these scrolls the five books of the Pentatuech and

131

give them to five children. I take another six children to whom I teach the six orders of the Mishna (Law). Then I tell each one, "Teach your section to your friends."

It was this work that Rabbi Yehuda the Prince had in mind when he said: "How great are the accomplishments of Rabbi Cheyah."

—Talmud, Kethuboth p. 103b

12. *For wisdom is a shelter as money is a shelter, and the advantage of knowledge is that wisdom preserves the life of those who possess it.*

There are times when both wisdom and wealth can bring protection. The story that follows illustrates that material possessions can be lost but wisdom remains a protective instrument.

A great scholar went on an ocean voyage with many merchants who were shipping and selling goods to distant lands. "Where is your merchandise?" the merchants asked the scholar. He answered, "My merchandise is more valuable than yours." The merchants looked all over the ship but could find no goods belonging to him. So they ridiculed the scholar.

On the way pirates attacked the passengers and robbed them of all their possessions. When the ship reached the harbor, the merchants found themselves with no money or goods. The scholar, however, made his way to a school and offered to teach. When the people discovered what a learned man he was, they showed him honor and respect and provided him with food, clothing and lodging. He was received by the officials of the city as a man of honor.

The merchants, his former fellow passengers, came to the scholar and asked forgiveness. They asked him to help them and intercede with the people to give them food.

They said, "Now we see that it was not mere boasting

when you told us that your merchandise was more valuable than ours."

—Midrash Tanchuma, Trumah 1:2

13. *Consider the work of God, for who can straighten what He has made bent.*

Who can straighten what He has made bent. Reflect deeply on God's rule. Whatever God has made is unchangeable.

Rabbi Eliezer ben Pdoss was very poor. Once when he had nothing to eat, he took the skin of a garlic and put it into his mouth. He became weak and fell asleep. The Rabbis who came to visit him noticed that he was crying and laughing in his sleep.

When he awoke they asked him, "Why did you cry and laugh?"

He replied that Divine Providence was sitting by his side. He said, "I asked how long will I suffer in this world?' And the answer came, 'Eliezer, my son, would you rather I remake the world? Perhaps you might be born at a happier hour.' I said, 'All this and then only perhaps!' I then asked, 'Which is the greater portion of my life, the part that I have already lived or the part I am still to live?' The reply was, 'The part that you have already lived.' Then I said, 'If so, I do not want it.' "

—Talmud, Taanith p. 25a

14. *In the day of good fortune enjoy yourself and in the the day of misfortune consider; God has ordained one to balance the other, to the end that man is unable to foresee his future.*

A heathen asked Rabbi Joshua, "Does not God foresee the future?"

"Yes," replied the Rabbi.

"Then why was God saddened when he had to bring a flood to destroy the world? Had he not foreseen this when he created man and delighted at the time?"

Rabbi Joshua asked the heathen, "Have you a son?"

"Yes," he answered.

"What did you do when he was born?"

He answered, "I rejoiced and invited my friends to rejoice with me."

"Didn't you know that your son will die some day?"

The heathen replied, "In time of joy, rejoice; in time of grief, grieve."

The Rabbi then told him, "God constructed the world, rejoicing in time of creation and saddened at the time of destruction."

—Midrash Rabbah, Genesis 27

15. *I have seen all things in my fleeting days, sometimes a just man perishes in spite of his justice and sometime a wicked man endures in spite of his wickedness.*

Sometimes a wicked man endures.

For three reasons God shows forbearance with the wicked in this world. One, perhaps they will repent. Two, perhaps they will do Mitzvohs (good deeds) for which God can reward them in this world. Three, perhaps upright children will descend from them.

History has proven this. God was long suffering with Ahaz (King of Judah, 577-561 B.C.E., who ruled for 16 years. He offered his own son to pass through fire worship and introduced idol worship—II Kings 12:3) from whom Hezekia (King of Judah, 561-532 B.C.E.) was a decendant. He ruled for 29 years, destroyed all idol worship and renewed the temple services and laws of Moses. (II Kings 18:3)

God was long suffering with Shimei (member of King Saul's family who cursed and conspired against King David —II Samuel 16:5) from whom Mordecai was descendant. (Mordecai was a hero of the Book of Esther, a steadfast Jew through whom Persian Jewry was saved.)

—Midrash Rabbah, Ecclesiastes 7:15

16. *Be not excessively righteous nor excessively wise, why should you be forsaken?*

Be not excessively righteous.

Be not more righteous than your Creator. As it is said in the case of Saul (I Samuel 15:5) who raised objections to the command to destroy Amalek. Saul said: "If the men have sinned, how have the women and children and the cattle, ox, and ass sinned?"

A heavenly voice declared: "Be not more righteous than your Creator."

Rabbi Shimon ben Lakish said: "Whoever shows himself merciful in circumstances where he should be without pity (there was a divine decree that the Amalekites, steeped in adultry and immorality be totally destroyed—I Samuel 15:3), in the end, he becomes without pity where he should be merciful. Saul was pitiless when he should have been merciful. (In the case of Nob, King Saul should have shown compassion—I Samuel 22:19.)

—Midrash Rabbah, Ecclesiastes 7:16

17. *Be not excessively wicked nor be a fool, why should you die before your time?*

Jeroboam sinned and caused others to sin, the sin of the many is attributed to him, as it is said: "For the sins of Jeroboam which he sinned and caused Israel to sin." (I Kings 15:30)

—Ethics of the Fathers 5:21

135

Then Jeroboam built Shechem in the hill-country of Ephraim and dwelt there. He went out from there and built Penuel. Jeroboam said to himself, "Now the kingdom will revert to the house of David. If this people go up to make sacrifices in the Temple of the Lord in Jerusalem, then will the heart of this people return to their lord, even to Rehoboam, king of Judah; and they will kill me, and return to Rehoboam, king of Judah."

So the king took counsel and made two calves of gold, and said to the people, "You have gone up to Jerusalem long enough. Behold your gods, O Israel, who brought you up from the land of Egypt."

So he set up the one in Bethel and the other he placed in Dan; and this thing became a sin for the people went to seek the one, even to Dan. He also made sanctuaries at high places, and made priests from among all sorts of people, who were not of the sons of Levi.

Jeroboam ordained a feast in the eighth month, on the fifteenth day of the month, like the feast that is in Judah, and went up to the altar; so he did in Bethel, sacrificing to the calves that he had made; and he stationed in Bethel the priests of the high places he had made.

And Jeroboam went up on the fifteenth day of the eighth month to the altar which he had made in Bethel, which he had devised of his own heart and he ordained a feast for the Israelites and went up to the altar to burn incense.

—I Kings 12:25-33

18. *It is well to grasp one and also do not let go of the other; for he who fears God will consider both.*

For he who fears God will consider both.

"And you should love the Lord your God with both, with your good and your evil inclinations."

The Rabbis interpret: "Behold it was good" (Genesis 1:25) the good impulse; "Behold it was very good" (Genesis 1:31) implies the impulse of evil."

Will you say the impulse of evil is "very good?"

But were it not for such inclinations, a man would not build a house, marry a wife, raise children or become involved in business affairs.

—Midrash Rabbah, Genesis 9

19. *Wisdom gives a wise man strength, more than ten rulers that were in a city.*

Wisdom gives a wise man strength.

Once Rabbi Tarfon said to Rabbi Akiva, "I will give you six hundred silver coins and buy me a field filled with God's blessings."

Rabbi Akiva replied, "I will do so."

Then Rabbi Akiva took the money and distributed it among the poor sages and brought bread and food for them. He told them that he would continue to buy food for them to rid them of worry for their sustenance.

Several months passed and Rabbi Tarfon met Rabbi Akiva and asked him, "Have you bought that field I had asked you about?"

"Yes," he replied.

Rabbi Tarfon asked him, "Is it a good or bad investment?"

Rabbi Akiva answered, "Your field is forever blessed. There is none like it in the entire land of Israel."

"Have you obtained a deed to the property from the former owner?"

Rabbi Akiva said, "Here I have it."

He took out the Book of Psalms and read to him, "He has distributed and given to the needy, his righteousness endures forever."

Rabbi Tarfon then said, "Indeed, this is the best property I have from all my possessions. Here, brother, is more money to continue to do good as you have done."

—Midrash Rabbah, Leviticus 34:16

20. *For no man on earth is righteous who always does good and never sins.*

Does good and never sins.

A man caught stealing was sentenced to be hanged. On the way to the gallows he said he had a wonderful secret that could make the country the richest in the world. He would discuss this secret only with the king. He told the king that it was a family secret; that he could plant a seed in the evening and it would bear fruit overnight.

The king arranged for the thief to demonstrate this miraculous experiment before many high officers of the government. The thief dug a hole and with the seed in his hand he approached the king. He said, "My lord, I have gone as far as I can. The actual planting must be done by one of absolute honesty. I, being a thief, cannot do it."

So the king turned to his prime minister who, frightened, whispered to the king that in his youth he had stolen something. The treasurer declined to do it. He said to the king, "I am in charge of thirty-three departments of state. I am afraid in my dealings I might have been dishonest about certain items. I better not do it."

The king summoned his minister of justice. The minister said his love of law was his success, but in his youth he had criminal tendencies. To overcome them he studied law and rose to his high position.

The king remained with the seed in his hand about to do the planting. He recalled that he once kept a necklace that belonged to his father. As the king too hesitated and did not plant the seed, the thief turned to him and said, "My lord, here are men in high positions who feel they have deviated and sinned. I only stole bread to eat. Should I be put to death for that?" The king gave him his pardon.

—Exempla of Rabbis, Gaster

21. *Furthermore, pay no attention to every word that is spoken lest you hear your servant insult you.*

Pay no attention to every word that is spoken.

A father who had three daughters met a father who had three sons. "You have three daughters and I have three sons. Let us make a match between them." But the father of the girls said, "I do not want to mislead you. My daughters each has a basic fault."

The father of the boys asked, "What are their vices?" The other replied, "one is a thief, the second is lazy and the third is a slanderer."

"If these are their vices I can cure them all." All three couples married. Following the weddings, the father-in-law gave the keys to all his treasures to the daughter who was a thief in order to satisfy her greed. To the second he gave many servants. To the third he tried to be kind and was eager to fulfill all her wishes so that she should not lie or slander anyone. He hoped by being good to her he would cure her habit of speaking evil.

Some time later the father came to see how his daughters were getting along. The first daughter said: "I want to thank you, my father, for this marriage for I get everything that my heart desires. In fact I have all the keys to the treasures in my hand so that I do not need to steal anything."

The second daughter told him, "I want to thank you, my father. Since I am married I need not do any work. I have plenty of servants. My husband and parents-in-law treat me well."

The third daughter said, "You think you are a good father! I thought you gave me one husband. As it is you gave me two, the father and the son. No sooner does my husband leave my house than my father-in-law comes in. He kisses me and hugs me and wants me to do his will. If you don't believe me, come tomorrow morning and you will see."

Next morning her father hid in the house. Her father-in-law came as usual, kissed and hugged her and asked, "How are you? Is there anything you want?" He did this with the good intention of curing her of her vice, but her father, believing his daughter's slander, rushed out and killed him.

Just then her two brothers-in-law came home and found their father dead and their father-in-law running away. They killed him. She began shouting, "Murder, Murder." They took this to mean that she was party to the killing and killed her too.

—Otzar Midrashim

22. *For you know in your heart that many times you yourself have insulted others.*

You yourself have insulted others.

The daughter of the Roman Emperor Hadrian said to Rabbi Joshua ben Chanania, "O, glorious wisdom in an ugly vessel." (You have great wisdom but you are so ugly.)

Rabbi Joshua replied, "Does your father keep his wine in earthen jars?"

She asked, "In what kind of vessel should he keep it?"

The Rabbi answered, "You are very rich. People like you ought to keep your wine in vessels of gold and silver."

So she went and told her father that it does not behoove a king to keep his wine in earthen jars like common men. He had the wine put into vessels of gold and silver and the wine turned sour. Then the emperor asked his daughter from whom she got this advice. She replied, "From Rabbi Joshua ben Chanania."

The emperor sent for the Rabbi and asked him, "What made you give my daughter such advice?"

The Rabbi replied, "As she spoke to me I spoke to her." The princess referred to his having great learning in an ugly vessel, so he inquired, "Why do you keep your wine in cheap vessels?"

The emperor said, "But there are many good-looking men who possess learning." Rabbi Joshua answered, "If these very people were ugly they would be still more learned."

—Talmud, Taanith p. 7a

23. *All this I tested with wisdom. I said, "I will be wise," but it was unattainable.*

But it was unattainable.

Why were the reasons for Biblical laws not disclosed. Because in two cases reasons were given and they caused the wisest man in the world to stumble. It was written: "He (a king) shall not provide himself with many wives so that his heart may not be estranged." (Deuteronomy 17:17) King Solomon said, "I will multiply wives and my heart will not be perverted." In the end we read, "When Solomon was old his wives turned away his heart." (I Kings 11:4)

Also it is wirtten: "He (a king) must not provide himself with many horses; not to enter into relations with Egypt." (Deuteronomy 17:16)

Solomon said: "I will provide myself with many horses but it will not cause a return to Egypt."

In the end we read, "And a chariot came up (for trading with Egypt) and went out of Egypt." (I Kings 10:29)

—Talmud, Sanhedrin p. 21b

24. *Inconceivable is that which exists and very mystifying, who can fathom it?*

Who can fathom it?

Just as the hand held before the eyes can hide the tallest mountain, so this small earthly life keeps our gaze from the vast radiance and the secrets that fill the world. And he who can draw the earthliness from before his eyes as one draws away the hand, will see the great light of the core of the world.

—Rabbi Nachman of Bratzlav

25. *I determined in my heart to study, to search and to seek wisdom and meaning; to learn that wickedness is folly and stupidity is madness.*

I determined in my heart to study.

A human being cannot be entirely good unless he knows evil. No one can evaluate pleasure unless he has tasted bitterness. Good is only the opposite of evil and pleasure is the antithesis of anxiety.

Man cannot express goodness if he has no evil inclination. God endowed man with the ability to do evil in order to enable him to do good, when he masters his evil nature. Without this evil inclination man could do no evil, but neither could he do good.

—Rabbi Pinchos of Koretz

26. *And I find more bitter than death the woman whose heart is snares and nets, her hands chains. He who is pleasing to God will escape her but the sinner will be trapped by her.*

The woman whose heart is snares.

The Almighty, in planning to fashion Eve from Adam's body, said: "I will not create her from his head, lest she be proud. I will not create her from his eyes, so that she should not be inquisitive. I will not create her from his ear lest she be eager to listen to gossip. I will not create her from his tongue so that she should not be talkative. If I create her from his heart she will be envious. If I create her from his hand, she will be grasping. If I create her from his foot, she will be a wanderer. Instead I will fashion her from an invisible part of man, so that even if he stands naked it cannot be seen."

Then God fashioned Eve from one of Adam's ribs and He said: "Be modest and chaste."

Nevertheless the result after all is that woman is proud, inquisitive, a gossip, talkative, a wanderer, grasping, and envious.

—Midrash Rabbah, Genesis 18

27. *Behold, this I have found, says Koheleth, adding one to one to reach a solution.*

Adding one to one.

As Akiva walked on the road he thought, I am forty years old and now it may be too late for me to study. Who knows if I will ever be able to achieve my goal and become a learned man? Suddenly he saw several shepherds sitting near a spring. At the mouth of the spring lay a stone which had many grooves. Akiva asked the shepherds, "What caused these grooves?"

They told him grooves were made by drops of water, drop by drop, that steadily dripped upon the stone. Akiva rejoiced at this reply and said: "If a stone can be affected by constant drops of water, how much easier should constant study be for me so that I may become a learned man."

He went together with his son and they came to an elementary teacher. Akiva said, "Master, teach us Torah." Rabbi Akiva took hold of one end of the tablet and his son of the other end of the tablet. The teacher wrote down, Aleph, Beth, for them and they learned it; the entire alphabet and they learned it; the Book of Leviticus and they learned it.

He went on studying until he learned the whole Bible. Then he went and appeared before Rabbi Eliezer and Rabbi Joshua. "My Masters," he said to them, "reveal the sense of Mishna (the code of law) to me." When they taught him one halacha (law) he went off to study by himself.

At the age of forty he began to study Torah. At the end of thirteen years, he taught Torah to multitudes.

—Avoth D'reb Nossan VI

28. *What I am still looking for but did not find; one man out of a thousand I found, but one woman among all these I have not found.*

One woman among all these I have not found.

Solomon, to prove this contention ordered his attendant to seek out a couple that was happily married and faithful to each other. Solomon ordered the husband to appear before him and said to him, "I learned that you are a good and wise man. I want to appoint you to the exalted office of Chief Overseer of my palace and to give you my daughter as a wife." He then told him that there was one condition attached to his offer. He must murder his wife that night; then he would be free to marry the King's daughter.

That day the husband came home but he was so full of pity for his wife he thought he could not kill her when she was awake. He decided that in the nightime when she is fast asleep he would kill her.

At night, the husband approached her bed with drawn sword. But as he saw his wife and the youngest child in her arms, he drew back and said, "I cannot murder my good wife even if the King offered me his entire Kingdom." In the morning the husband returned to the King and told him his decision.

Some time elapsed and King Solomon called for the wife to appear before him. The King said to her, "My dear woman, my love for you is very deep. I want to marry you. Now you must murder your husband and become my wife." The King gave her an imitation sword which looked like steel. The woman took the sword to carry out the King's wish.

At night she got up and seeing her husband fast asleep she drew the "sword" and struck her husband. The "sword" did no harm. Awakened, he saw his wife standing over him holding the implement. She confessed her evil plan. The next day both husband and wife were summoned to the King to tell their story and confirm the teaching of this verse.

—Otzar Midrashim

29. *Behold, this only have I discovered, that God made man upright but they have sought many devices.*

The chapter concludes with the assertion that God created man with many good qualities. In time man abused his capabilities. It is not God but man who is to be blamed for man's degeneration.

This can be compared to a King who had a golden statue in his own likeness placed in front of his palace. A bird rested upon it and soiled it. So God made man upright. The evil impulse arose and corrupted him. The Psalmist expresses this: "I thought you were angels, that you were all sons of the Most High. Yet you shall die as men do and fall like any prince."

—Midrash Tanchuma, Genesis 7

CHAPTER EIGHT

1. *Who can compare with the wise man? And who knows the interpretation of an event? A man's wisdom illumines his face and the harshness of his features is changed.*

A man's wisdom illumines his face.

This refers to a Rabbinical scholar, in two contrasting situations. "A man's wisdom illumines his face" (when he is asked a question and is able to answer). "And the harshness of his features is changed" (when he is asked a question and is unable to answer). Rabbi Abbahu visited Caesarea and when he came back his face was shining. The disciples of Rabbi Yochanan told their Rabbi: "Rabbi Abbahu must have discovered a treasure."

The Rabbi asked, "Why do you say this?"

They replied, "His face is shining."

The Rabbi said to them, "Maybe he discovered something new in the Torah."

The disciples went and asked him, "Have you learned a new point of Torah?"

He answered them, "In Caesarea I heard an ancient interpretation of the Mishna (Law Code) which applied to the text, 'A man's wisdom illumines his face.' "

—Midrash Rabbah, Ecclesiastes 8:1

2. *I obey the King's command because of the oath
taken before God.*

Obey the king's command.

Why are men likened to fish? Just as a larger fish in the
sea swallows the smaller, so also is it with man. If not for
the fear of government the stronger men would overpower
and oppress the weaker.

This is what the Mishna taught when Rabbi Chanina,
the Vice High Priest said, "Pray for the welfare of the
government, for were it not for fear of the government, men
would swallow each other alive."

—Talmud, Avoda Zarah p. 4a

3. *Do not hurry to leave his presence; do not persist in
a bad cause, for he does whatever he pleases.*

Do not hurry to leave his presence.

A king once had to entrust someone with a very important
and challenging mission. He wished to appoint one out of
three candidates but only after testing their character and
courage. The king asked each to tell him the most significant
experience in his life.

The first told of this incident: He once saw a person
drowning in a river. Without a moment's hesitation he im-
pulsively jumped to save him. It took a great deal of daring
to rescue the drowning man.

The second candidate related that he was walking in a
quiet street. He found a bag of money. There was nobody
around and he could easily have kept silent about his find
that would have made him a very rich man. Instead he took
the money to the police and the owner was traced. The king
was impressed with his honesty and trustworthiness.

The third candidate said he had no spectacular experience to relate except a family episode. One day his father
brought home a bunch of cords and asked his five children

to untangle it. He needed the cords soon and there were hundreds of knots to undo. "We all sat down to the job. Soon my two brothers and two sisters gave up. They became bored and tired with such a monotonous assignment. This job to them was uninteresting and unenjoyable. Only I remained at it. I worked until I undid all the knots. It was a challenge to complete the assignment."

—Bnai Yisrael, Pekuday

4. *Inasmuch as the word of the king is supreme; and who can say to him, "What are you doing?"*

Who can say to him,
What are you doing?

A sick lion had developed bad breath. In the forest he met a donkey.

"Does my breath smell?" the lion asked.

"It surely does," replied the donkey.

"How dare a simpleton like you insult the king of all animals!" roared the lion, and fell upon the donkey devouring him. Then he saw a bear. "Does my breath smell?" the lion asked.

"Oh no, your breath smells sweeter than honey," said the bear.

"You liar, how dare you lie to me," he roared and devoured the bear.

Then he saw a fox. "Smell my breath and tell me whether my breath is sweet."

The fox answered, "Forgive me, O king of the forest, for I am unable to smell. I have a severe cold."

—Ahavath Dodim

5. *He who obeys the commandments will experience no harm; and a wise heart senses the time and judgment.*

149

He who obeys the commandments will experience no harm.

Once a pious man was praying by the roadside. A high rank-ing officer went by and greeted him, but he did not return the greeting. The officer waited until he finished his prayers.

As he concluded his prayers the officer said to him, "In-solent man, doesn't your law teach you not to endanger your life? Why didn't you return my greeting when I greet-ed you? If I had killed you with my sword, who would have demanded your blood from me?"

The pious man answered, "Be patient and I will justify my conduct. If you, sir, were standing before a human king and someone would pass by and greet you, would you re-spond with a greeting?"

"No," he answered.

"If you did respond to his greeting what would have hap-pened to you?"

"The king would have killed me," was the reply.

The pious man then said to him, "If you would have acted in this way standing before a human king, who is here today and dead tomorrow, how much more should I have so behaved, when standing before the Supreme King of Kings, the Holy One, Blessed be He, who is Eternal and lives for ever and ever."

The officer was pleased with this explanation and the pious man returned to his home in peace.

—Talmud, Berochoth p. 32b

6. *For every matter has its time and judgment, for the tyranny of man is heavy upon him.*

For every matter has its time.

King David called his chief jeweler and ordered him to fashion a ring for him so that when he would look at it when sad, he would turn happy, and when happy, he would turn sad.

The craftsman went home puzzled and frustrated. He did not know how he could fashion such a magical instrument.

Young Solomon on seeing the jeweler, asked him why he looked so sad and apprehensive. The jeweler told the prince about his father, the King's extraordinary request. Solomon advised him to make a ring and inscribe on it, "This too shall pass."

—Oral Tradition

7. *For no one knows what shall be, for who can tell him when it shall be?*

A poor man who lived in a one-room hut came to a Rabbi for advice. He reported that his wife and children constantly quarreled because of lack of room. "It is no longer a home."

The Rabbi listened and considered this problem. The Rabbi said: "Will you promise to do as I tell you? You mentioned that you have some domestic animals and chickens in your yard. Take them all into your house to live with you."

The poor man could not see the logic of this advice but he did as he was told. Early next morning he ran back to the Rabbi and cried, "Rabbi, what have you done to me. I did as you told me. My house has turned into a barn."

"If that is the case," said the Rabbi, "go home and move the chickens out of your house." The man went home and did so.

The next day he returned to the Rabbi complaining that with the cow inside the house had become a stable. It is impossible for us to live with that animal!

"Go home," said the Rabbi, "and take the cow out of your house. God will help you."

Next day the man returned to the Rabbi in a happy mood. "Rabbi, your advice worked. Life has become pleasant and bearable. With all the animals out of my house it has become so orderly and quiet. Now I have a real home."

—Old Parables

8. *No man has power over his spirit to restrain the spirit, neither has he control over the day of death; no substitute can be sent into battle, neither will evil schemes rescue its owners.*

Neither has he control over the day of death.

King David asked, "Lord of the Universe, let me know when I will die."

"It is a decree before me, that no mortal should know his last day."

"And the measure of my days, what is it?" prayed David

"It is decreed before me not to reveal to any man the number of years he is to live."

"Tell me when I will cease." (On what day of the week will I die.)

And God answered, "You will die on a Sabbath."

"Let me die a day after Sabbath," King David pleaded.

"No, for the rule of your son Solomon shall already have become due after that day, and the kingdom of one must not overlap that of the other for even one second."

"Then let me die a day before that Sabbath," asked King David.

God answered, "No man may die before his hour comes. Better is to me the Torah you will study for one single day than the thousand sacrifices your son Solomon is destined to offer on my altar."

—Talmud, Sabbath p. 30a

9. *All this I have seen and I have applied my heart to everything that happened under the sun, at a time when man has power to harm his fellow man.*

When man has power to harm his fellow man.

Emperor Hadrian saw a Jew walking past him. The Jewish man greeted him, saying, "Long live the Emperor!"

"Who are you," asked the Emperor.

"I am a Jew," he answered.

"How dare you, a Jew, to greet me. Kill him!" the Emperor ordered his guards.

Another Jew who saw the incident decided not to greet the Emperor.

The Emperor called this Jew over to him and asked him also, "Who are you?"

"I am a Jew," was the answer.

"How dare you, a Jew, walk by without greeting me. Kill him!" he ordered his soldiers.

One of the officers asked the Emperor, "I don't understand your actions. If you kill one Jew because he greeted you, why did you do the same thing to the second Jew because he did not greet you?"

Emperor Hadrian answered, "Are you trying to teach me how to handle those I hate?"

—Midrash Rabbah, Lamentation 3

10. *And so I have seen wicked men buried and they came to rest, and those who did right depart from the place of the holy and were forgotten in the city. This too is vanity.*

I have seen wicked men buried.

On the same day a good pious scholar, and a wicked tax collector, died. When both bodies were brought to the cemetery to be buried, robbers invaded the grounds. All the people ran away before the two were buried.

One devoted disciple of the scholar returned to guard the coffin of his teacher. The next day the people returned to complete the burial. They mistook the body of the tax collector for that of the scholar.

The friends of the tax collector took the body of the sage and buried him in the grave prepared for the tax collector.

The young student went home sad and troubled over this dishonor to his teacher. At night the Rabbi came, in a dream, to his disciple. He said: "Do not grieve! I am destined to Paradise and the wicked one will receive his punishment. Once I heard someone slandering a scholar and I did not protest, therefore I suffered this shame."

The tax collector had once arranged a banquet for the governor, who could not attend. The tax collector took the food and distributed it to the poor. That is why he received his reward.

—Rashi, Talmud, Sanhedrin p. 44b

11. *Because the sentence against crime is not promptly executed, that is why man's heart is inclined to do evil.*

The fact that punishment does not immediately follow the sin misleads people to believe that there will be no punishment. They are inclined to think they can sin with impunity.

Titus the wicked blasphemed heaven incredibly. What did he do? He brought a harlot into the Holy of Holies, spread out a scroll and committed a sin there. He then took a curtain and put all the vessels of the sanctuary in it and took them aboard ship to return triumphantly home.

A storm sprang up at sea which threatened to drown him. Titus then said, "Evidently the power of their God is only on the water. Pharaoh was drowned in water; Sisera was drowned in water; now he is trying to drown me in water. If He is really all powerful let Him come and fight me on dry land."

A heavenly voice said: "Sinner, son of a sinner, I have a tiny creature in my world, a wasp. Go up on dry land and fight with it."

When Titus reached harbor a wasp entered his nose. It buzzed within his head for seven years.

—Talmud, Gittin p. 56b

12. *Even though the sinner does wrong a hundred times and his punishment is delayed, nevertheless I know it will be well with the God-fearing who revere God.*

The delay in punishment, even to a constant sinner, does not shake the author's faith in the system of retribution and reward.

A hungry lion met a fox who sensed that the lion was ready to devour him. Said the fox, "I am concerned that his majesty, the king of all animals, have an adequate meal. I am a lean animal. There stands a fat man. There you will have a good meal."

"I am afraid," said the lion, "since the man is engaged in prayer and God will punish me."

"This should not deter you," answered the fox. "The Bible speaks of God punishing the third and fourth generations. Why worry now?"

The idea of the postponed judgment of God appealed to the lion. He ran towards the man and fell into a ditch. The lion called to the fox for help, as he dangled in pain over a deep ditch. "You said God punished the third or fourth generation and here I am punished."

Replied the fox cunningly, "It may be that your grandfather sinned and you are suffering for his sins."

—Rav Hai Gaon

13. *And it shall not be well with the wicked but like a shadow, he shall not prolong his days because he does not fear God.*

The following story illustrates that the prosperity of the wicked is only transitory as a shadow and an illusion.

155

A farmer had an old donkey, a young donkey, and a pig. The farmer would strictly ration food for the donkeys, but the pig he would offer food without limit.

The young donkey asked the mother, "How is it while we who do all the work for our owner, he gives us little food and the pig does nothing and gets all the food."

The mother replied, "Do not envy the pig. The time will come and you will see why this pig is fattened."

The festival came and the farmer killed the pig. The young donkey went about his work with more spirit and more understanding.

—Midrash Rabbah, Esther 7

14. *There is an illusion that exists on earth: sometimes just men are treated according to the conduct of the wicked and sometimes wicked men are treated according to the conduct of the just. I said that this too is an illusion.*

The following story illustrates this verse. Rabbi Joshua found Elijah the Prophet treating the just as if they were wicked and the wicked as if they were just.

Rabbi Joshua ben Levi and Elijah the Prophet were traveling together. They reached the home of the poor man whose entire fortune consisted of one cow. The family was cordial and gave them food and lodging.

In the morning, Elijah prayed that the cow would die. The cow, the only possession of the family, expired.

In the evening they arrived at the home of a very rich man who refused to receive them. Elijah uttered a blessing and a prayer that a broken wall be miraculously rebuilt in this house.

In the evening they came to a Synagogue where they were received most discourteously. Elijah blessed the congregation and prayed that they all become leaders.

The next day they went to another Synagogue where they were received with honor and respect. The people provided a feast and lodging for them. On leaving, Elijah the Prophet blessed them and said: "May the Lord grant you only one leader."

Rabbi Joshua could no longer suffer the unfair and unjust treatment by Elijah the Prophet. Elijah said, "Now I can explain all that seemed so unjust and unreasonable to you. That day the hostess in the poor family was to die, and I prayed the cow die in her place.

"In the house of that rich man there lies buried a great treasure. If the rich man were to rebuild the wall himself he would have discovered that fortune. The congregation that mistreated us I wished that they all become leaders. For then, they will always have strife that will lead to destruction. For the congregation that received us well, I prayed for one leader who would coordinate their activities and unite the people in harmony."

—Sefer Massioth, L'Rabbinu Nissim Gaon

15. *And I praised enjoyment because a man has nothing better under the sun than to eat and to drink and be happy and have this accompany him in his toil, during the span of his life allotted to him by God under the sun.*

The author presents a rule of life: Cultivate happiness and enjoy life's gifts because they are God given. All pleasure is recommended if it is in a moral setting.

What labors Adam had to perform before he obtained bread to eat. He had to plow; he had to sow; he had to reap. He then bound, threshed, and selected the ears. He then ground and sifted the flour, kneaded and baked. At last he ate. In contrast, I get up and find all that done for me.

How many activities Adam had to perform before he obtained a garment to wear. He sheared, washed the wool, combed it, spun it and wove it. Then at last he had clothes to wear.

In contrast I get up and find all these activities done for me. Ben Zoma used to say: What does a good guest say? How much effort my host has exerted for me. How much meat he has provided for me. How much wine he has provided for me. How much care he has given me. And all his effort was only for my sake. But what does a bad guest say? After all, how much has my host done for me? I have eaten one piece of meat; I drank one cup of wine. The effort my host made was only for his wife and children.

—Talmud, Berochoth p. 58a

16. *I set my heart to study wisdom and to consider the activity which takes place on earth; even to deprive oneself of sleep day and night.*

Koheleth returns again to face the riddle of life. He is willing to search for an answer day and night. This story presents King David speculating and questioning certain aspects of existence.

King David questioned the value of the existence of certain creatures. He wondered what good were wasps, spiders and fools. Later his life was saved by each of them.

David said that all the world was good and beautiful with the exception of insanity.

What use can the world derive from lunatics and fools?

It happened that David, on his flight from King Saul, came to Achish, King of the Philistines. The bodyguards of the King, brothers of Goliath, demanded that David, who killed their brother, be executed.

In his distress David prayed to God to let him appear as a madman in the eyes of the King and his court. The wife and daughter of King Achish were both deranged. That is why the King said: "Do I lack madmen, that ye have brought this fellow in my presence?" This was how David was rescued.

Once David expressed his wonder why God formed such apparently useless creatures as spiders. They do nothing but spin webs that have no value.

On one occasion he had taken refuge in a cave. King Saul and his guards were in pursuit of him. They were about to enter that cave when God sent a spider to weave its web across the opening. King Saul told his men to turn from the fruitless search in this cave, for the spider's web was the best proof that no one had passed through its entrance.

There was a time when David scorned wasps and mosquitoes. What good are they to the world except to breed maggots.

It happened that David surprised King Saul and his guards while they were asleep in their camp. David decided to take a pitcher that stood near General Abner. As David passed to get the pitcher, Abner's knees were drawn up, but as David was returning Abner stretched out his feet which pinned David to the spot where he stood. David's life was in great danger, but a wasp stung Abner, who without waking, moved his leg and released David.

—Midrash Tehillim 34

17. *I realized that it is all the work of God. Man cannot comprehend the meaning of that which happens under the sun. No matter how much a man will labor to seek it, he will not fathom it; and even if a wise man should determine to know he will not be able to grasp it.*

The chapter closes with an affirmative statement that there is design in the universe. Man has neither the physical endurance nor the mental capacity to comprehend the totality of the divine government of the universe.

A king held a discussion with one of his most distinguished subjects. The king asked him: "What were you doing?"

The man replied, "I was thinking that in comparison with the highest sphere our planet earth is no more than a swampy region in a great sea. For even the earth is not totally inhabited but a little more than a quarter. Even in the inhabited portion you will find that the northern part is uninhabited. And then, even in the inhabited portion, there are mountains and hills, seas and rivers, deserts, forests and wilderness.

"How comparatively small is the inhabited part of the earth. I am in one of the innumerable cities. In that very city there are shops, streets and market places. I am in one spot only. I am no more than a fragment of the place in which I dwell. If so small is my portion in this world, and this whole world is a little part of the universal plan of the Creator, how can I comprehend His Presence and His mysteries."

—Shimon ben Zemach Duran

CHAPTER NINE

1. *For all this I took to heart to clarify all this, that the just and the wise and their actions are in God's hands; man does not know whether he will be in favor or disfavor. All is ordained before them.*

The author concedes that the course of divine providence is inexplicable. Man is unable to predict good or bad; either may occur.

Rabbi Akiva was traveling and he came to a certain town. He looked for lodging but was refused everywhere. He said, "Whatever God does is for the best."

He spent the night in an open field. He had with him a hen, a donkey, and a lamp. A strong wind came and blew out the lamp; a weasel came and ate the hen; a lion came and devoured the donkey. Even then he said, "Whatever God does is for the best."

The same night robbers came and captured the inhabitants of the town. He later remarked, "Did I not say, 'Whatever God does is for the best.'"

The light of the lamp and sounds of the hen and donkey would have betrayed his presence to the robbers.

—Talmud, Berochoth p. 60b

2. The same fate awaits all. One event to the just and the unjust; to the good and to the clean and to the unclean; to the one who sacrifices and the one who does not sacrifice. As is the good, so is the sinner; he who takes an oath as he who fears an oath.

The same fate awaits all.

The world has been compared to a shop, because like a shop, many things of a different nature are found in it. Some are bitter, some are sweet, some are hot, some are cold; some are liquid, some are dry; some are solid, some are soft; and the choice is left to the purchaser and it is within his power that his acts be either evil or good, little or much.

—Rabbi Menachem ben Shlomo Ha-Me'eri

3. This is an evil in all that is done under the sun, that there is one fate for all. Therefore the heart of man is full of evil, madness is in their minds while they live and after that they join the dead.

That there is one fate for all.

The Mishna teaches: "And all is prepared for the banquet." Why is death called a "banquet?" To teach the idea that when people are invited to a banquet they all enter through one door. But when they sit down they do not sit down in an unsystematic manner, but everyone according to his position and dignity. So too, departing from the world is the fate of everyone, of the righteous and the wicked. But only in accordance with his achievements does each one receive the reward which is coming to him for his labors.

—*Machzor Vitry*

4. For he who is classed among the living has hope, for a live dog is better than a dead lion.

The living has hope.

A man was carrying a heavy load on his shoulders. He grew weary, tired and hopeless. He dropped his heavy burden and wept over his fate and cried bitterly, "I cannot bear this life any longer. Death, come and take me!"

Immediately the Angel of Death came and asked, "Did you call for me? What do you want?"

Frightened to see the messenger of death, the man answered, "Please help me place the load back on my shoulders."

—Harvard Classics

5. *For the living know that they will die but the dead know nothing; they no longer receive reward. Even their memory is forgotten.*

They no longer receive reward.

Rabbi Tanchum of Neway said: "Solomon, where is your wisdom and where is your understanding? Not only do your words contradict the words of your father David, but they are self-contradictory. Your father David said, 'The dead cannot praise the Lord' (Psalms 115:7), while you said, 'I regard as more fortunate the dead who have already died.' (Ecclesiastes 4:2) Yet again you said, 'For a live dog is better than a dead lion.' " (Ecclesiastes 9:4)

What King David said can be understood without difficulty. David said, "The dead cannot praise the Lord." This is what he meant. Let a man always study Torah and do good deeds before he dies. As soon as he dies he is free from the practice of Torah and good deeds and God receives no praise from him.

Rabbi Yochanan said: "What does the verse in the Psalms (86:6) mean? 'Among the dead I am free?' Once a person dies he becomes free of the Torah and good deeds."

—Talmud, Sabbath p. 30a

6. *Their loves, their hates and their jealousies have already perished; they have no further share forever in all that happens under the sun.*

Their loves, their hates and their jealousies have already perished.

There the wicked cease from troubling; there the weary are at rest.
The prisoners rest together. They hear not the voice of the taskmaster.
The small and the great are there, and the slave is free from his master.

—Job 3:17, 18, 19

7. *Go, eat your bread with joy and drink your wine with a happy heart, for God has already approved your actions.*

God has already approved your actions.

Abba Tachna the Pious was approaching his city. He was coming home on Friday before dark with his bundle on his shoulders. He found a sick man full of boils lying on the road. The sick man said to him, "Rabbi, you will do a charitable thing if you will carry me to the city."

The Rabbi thought, if I leave my pack of goods I will lose my source of sustenance for my family. But if I leave this sorely afflicted man, I will commit a deadly sin."

What did he do? He made his good impulse master the evil impulse and carried the sick man into the city. After that, he went back for his bundle of goods and came back into the city at sunset. Everybody wondered, could this be Abba Tachna the Pious carrying a pack of goods at sunset so close to the Sabbath?

He himself was disturbed. He said: "Maybe I am violating the Sabbath!"

Miraculously the sun re-appeared.

He still felt troubled. A heavenly voice said to him: "Go, eat your bread with joy, and drink your wine with a happy heart, for God has already approved your actions.

—Midrash Rabbah, Ecclesiastes 9:7

8. *Let your garments always be white and your head never lack ointment.*

Let your garments always be white.

Rabbi Yehudah the Prince asked: "To what may this text be compared?" A king planned a feast to which he invited guests. He conveyed a message to them: Go wash yourselves, anoint yourselves with oil, iron your clothes and prepare yourselves for the feast. But he had set no date for the event.

The wise guests thought the feast may be called at any time because a king's palace does not lack anything. They therefore stayed near the palace. The foolish guests did not mind the general invitation. They thought, we will be notified when the feast is to take place, for there cannot be a large banquet without preparation. So the plasterer went on with his plastering, the potter to work clay, the smith over his oven of coals, the washer of clothes to his laundry.

Suddenly the king commanded: "Let them all come to the feast."

The waiters hurried the guests. As a result some came dressed in their best clothes and some in their dirty clothes. The king was pleased with the wise guests who respected his invitation and added splendor to the banquet. He was displeased with the foolish guests who did not pay adequate attention to his invitation and disgraced the palace.

The king gave the order, "Let those who prepared themselves for the feast come and eat of the king's feast, but those who are not adequately prepared shall not eat of the royal meal.

—Midrash Rabbah, Ecclesiastes 9:8

9. *Enjoy life with the woman you love, all the fleeting days of your life which He has given you under the sun, throughout your brief days, for that is your share in life and for all the effort of your toil under the sun.*

A man who has no wife lives without joy, without blessing and without goodness.

—Talmud, Yevomoth p. 62b

Once three poor men each expressed a wish. The first wanted to be rich, the second wanted to become a scholar and the third wanted a good wife.

Elijah came and gave a gold coin to the first man on the condition that he would remain meek and charitable. To the second he gave a book on the condition that he study and teach others. The third he recommended to a woman who appeared bad tempered, but in reality was a good woman.

Years later Elijah came back to test them.

He took five orphans to the rich man and asked assistance in ransoming their mother from the hand of robbers. He was refused. The next day he removed his blessing and the man became poor.

He then brought the children to the scholar and asked him to keep them and to teach them. He was refused. He then took back his book which he had earlier given him and the scholar began to forget his learning and died in misery.

Elijah then went to the man with the good wife and he was well received. She gave them the last remaining food in the house. She then went to meet her husband and told him that a worthy old man was in the house. She asked him not to be angry that there was no food left, since she had fed the guests. She persuaded him to kill their only calf to feed the weary travelers.

Elijah rewarded them by giving them the money and wisdom he had taken from the other two.

—Exempla of Rabbis

Even after ten years of childlessness, a married couple must still not neglect their duty of begetting children.

Rabbi Idi tells that such a couple of Sidon after ten years of marriage and still childless came to Rabbi Shimon Ben Yochoee to be parted.

The Rabbi said to them: "I beg that just as you were joined in a festive manner let your separation also be preceded with festivity. They accepted his counsel and planned the celebration of an elaborate meal accompanied with much drinking. In the midst of this joyous mood the husband said to his wife: "My daughter, choose any article that you desire from this household and take it with you to your father's house."

What did she do? As he fell asleep she ordered the servants to place him on a couch and carry him to her father's house.

At midnight, the effects of the wine had worn off and he awoke, and said to his wife, "Where am I?" She replied, "You are in my father's house." "But why am I in your father's house?" She answered: "Didn't you say to me last night 'Choose any choice article from our household and take it with you?' There is nothing in the world that I prefer more than you."

They again went to Rabbi Shimon Ben Yochoee who prayed for them and they became fertile.

—Midrash, Song of Songs 1

10. *Whatever you are able to achieve do while you have strength, for there is no action nor plan, no knowledge nor wisdom in the grave where you are going.*

Do while you have strength.

Before the sage Mar Ukba died he requested, "Bring me a list of my charities." He found that seven thousand gold coins were entered in his book. He said, "The provisions are little and the journey is long." He immediately distributed half his wealth.

The Talmud asks how could he do that? Has not Rabbi Elai said, "It has been taught at Usha that if a man wishes to give liberally he should not give away more than one-fifth of his wealth?"

The anwser is that this applies only during a man's lifetime, since excessive generosity may cause him to become poor. But at the time of death there is no limit to giving charity.

—Talmud, Kethuboth p. 67b

11. *Again I observed under the sun that the race is not to the swift nor the battle to the brave, nor is there bread for the wise, nor riches for the intelligent, nor favor for scholars, for all are victims of time and chance.*

Nor is there bread for the wise.

Once Rabbi Gamliel and Rabbi Joshua travelled on a ship. Rabbi Gamliel took along only bread. Rabbi Joshua took along bread and flour. When Rabbi Gamliel no longer had any bread he had to depend on the flour that Rabbi Joshua had. Rabbi Gamliel asked, "Did you prepare flour because you anticipated a delay in our trip?"

Rabbi Joshua answered him, "Once every seventy years a certain star appears. The sailors not knowing this may steer on a wrong course. I suspected the appearance of this star (Halley's Comet) that it would mislead the captain of this ship."

"You possess so much wisdom and still you must travel by ship (to earn a livelihood)," said Rabbi Gamliel.

Rabbi Joshua said to him, "You marvel at my wisdom. You would be extremely astonished at the wisdom of two Sages you have on land. Rabbi Eliezer ben Chisman and Rabbi Yochanan ben Gudgada are so learned that they can calculate how many drops of water there are in the sea, yet they are so poor that they have neither bread nor clothing to wear."

—Talmud, Horioth p. 10a

12. *Furthermore, man never knows his time, like fish caught in an evil net, as birds trapped in a snare, so men are trapped in an hour of calamity as it falls upon them suddenly.*

Like fish caught in an evil net.

Everything is given on a pledge (of good conduct). A net is spread for all the living (no one can evade it, if he sins). The shop is open and the storekeeper gives credit; the account book is open; the hand writes and whoever wishes to borrow may come and borrow. But the collectors (suffering and sickness) regularly make their daily rounds and exact payment from man, whether it is with his will, or against his will, and they have that on which they can rely since the judgment is just.

—Ethics of the Fathers 3:20

13. *This also I saw as a bit of wisdom under the sun and it greatly impressed me.*

I saw as a bit of wisdom.

Once there was a man of great learning in science and medicine. One day he fell sick. He had to leave his home to move to a warmer climate. He settled in a small town among simple and poor people. When he was asked by the

169

townspeople, "What is your calling?" he said, "I am a country doctor."

His wife asked him, "I can't understand how a great doctor like you with so many accomplishments should say that you are a country doctor. What kind of honor or profit do you expect from that?"

He explained, "The people of this town are poor people with simple needs. All my scholarly and professional abilities are of no use to them. To them the most useful and important medical help is the simple remedies that a small country doctor can offer them.

—Dubno Maggid

14. *There was a small city with few men in it and a powerful king came and surrounded it and built great siege works over it.*

A powerful king came and surrounded it.

King Alexander of Macedonia said to the wise men: "I am going to the land of Africa." They told him you cannot go there because there are mountains of darkness on the way.

"That will not deter me from going," he declared.

"That was not what I asked you. Tell me what to do to get there."

They said to him, "You take Libyan donkeys that travel in the dark. Then take a rope and tie it along the side of the road so it will guide you to your destination and on your return."

He followed their instructions and started his trip. He arrived at a place where there were only women. He declared war and besieged them.

The women said to him, "If you kill us, people will say that he killed women and if we kill you, you will be known as the king who was killed by women."

When the king left he wrote on the gate of that city: "I,

Alexander of Macedonia was a fool till I came to the city
of women in Africa and I learned wisdom from the women."

—Talmud, Tammid p. 32a

15. *Now, there was found in it a poor, wise man, who by
his wisdom rescued the city. Yet no one remembered that
poor man.*

By his wisdom rescued the city.

And they came and besieged Abel-beth-maacah. They threw
up a mound against the city, for it stood even with the ram-
part; and all the people with Joab battered the wall to
throw it down.

Now a wise woman out of the city called, "Hear, hear!
Say, I pray you, Joab, come here that I may speak to you."

So he came near her; and the woman said, "Are you
Joab?"

"I am," he answered.

"Listen to the words of your maid-servant," she said to
him.

"I am listening," he replied.

Then she said, "They used to say, 'Let them take counsel at Abel,' and so a matter was settled. I am of those who
are peaceable and faithful in Israel. You seek to destroy a
city and a mother of Israel; why will you destroy the heritage of the Lord?"

Then Joab answered and said, "Far be it, far be it from
me that I should destroy or devastate! That is not the case.
But a man of the hill-country of Ephraim, Sheba, the son of
Bichri, by name, has lifted up his hand against King David;
only deliver him up, and I will withdraw from the city."

"Behold, his head shall be thrown to you from the wall,"
said the woman to Joab. Then the woman went in her wisdom to all the people. And they cut off the head of Sheba,
the son of Bichri, and threw it down to Joab. He blew the

171

trumpet and they were dispersed from the city, each to his home. And Joab returned to Jerusalem, to the king.

—II Samuel 20:15-22

16. *So I reflected, wisdom is better than strength, yet the poor man's wisdom is despised and his words are not accepted.*

The poor man's wisdom is despised.

The government of Rome issued a decree forbidding Jews to study the Torah. Pappas ben Yehudah found that Rabbi Akiva was establishing public lectures and teaching Torah. He said to Rabbi Akiva, "Aren't you afraid of the government?"

He replied, "To explain let me tell you a parable. A fox walked on the bank of a river. He saw fishes swimming and swarming from one place to another. The fox asked them, 'Why are you running?' The fish replied, 'We are running away from the nets cast for us by the fisherman.'

"The fox asked them, 'Would you like to come ashore and we shall live peacefully together the way my ancestors lived with your ancestors.' The fish replied, 'Are you the one who is thought to be the cleverest of all animals? Surely you are not clever but foolish. If we are afraid of our lives in the place where we live, what can we expect if we move into an element in which we would die.' So it is with our people. If this is our plight when we sit and study the Torah which is the foundation of our life, can you imagine what would happen to us if we were to abandon the Torah?"

—Talmud, Berochoth p. 61a

17. *The words of the wise spoken softly are more acceptable than the shouting of the king of fools.*

Words of the wise spoken softly.

God revealed Himself on Mount Sinai rather than on

any of the other mountains because it is the smallest mountain of all. For when God decided to give the Torah to Israel, all the mountains began boastfully saying one to the other, "I am taller than you. Upon me God will give the Torah.

When the Creator saw how they were all bragging, He said to them: "Why do you envy high mountains, mountains which God has desired for His abode?"

God said to Mount Tabor, Hermon and Carmel, "Why are you quarreling with each other? I shall give the Torah only from Mount Sinai because it is the smallest mountain and I love him who is humble."

—Rabbi David Hanagid

18. *Wisdom is better than weapons of war but one sinner destroys much good.*

One sinner destroys much good.

A man should ever regard himself as if he were half guilty and half deserving merit. If he does one precept, he will feel happy for balancing the weight of the scale towards merit. If he commits a sin, he should feel the pain for balancing the weight in the scale towards guilt, for it is written, "one sinner destroys much good." On account of one sin which he does he loses much reward.

Rabbi Eliezer, son of Rabbi Shimon said, "The world is judged by the greater measure of deeds (good or bad) and an individual is judged by the greater measure of his deeds (good or bad). If one does one good deed, he should be happy for he is tipping the scale for both himself and for the world on the side of merit. If he commits one sin, he should feel the pain for he is tipping the scale for himself and the entire world in the balance of guilt. For it is said, 'one sinner destroys much good.' On account of one single sin which this man commits, he and the entire world lose much reward."

—Talmud, Kidushin p. 40a

CHAPTER TEN

1. *As dead flies befoul and corrupt the perfumer's ointment, so a little folly can outweigh wisdom and honor.*

A little folly can outweigh wisdom and honor.

An architect once asked his apprentice to make an exact
copy of a blueprint. He warned him to be careful in every
detail since it was to be drawn on an extremely reduced
scale.

The apprentice drew the copy and made every effort
to reproduce the plan very accurately. When he finished he
presented his work to the architect, who examined the copy.
At first he was rather pleased with the neat and meticulous
appearance of the drawing. Suddenly he turned to the apprentice in anger and shouted, "You idiot, you failed to put
in one small dot that is on the original. How could you leave
out that dot?"

The apprentice asked his employer why he was so up-
set by such a small mistake.

"Don't you understand," the architect told him, "that
little dot represents one of the pillars which is to support
the entire upper floor. If this pillar is omitted the entire
plant would collapse. It may seem a mere small dot on the
reduced blueprint, but in reality it represents a basic part
of the building."

—Dubno Maggid

2. *A wise man's heart keeps him to the right and a fool's to the left.*

A wise man's heart keeps him to the right.

A king owned a large and precious ruby. One day, through an accident the ruby became scratched. The king offered a great reward to any skilled diamond cutter or craftsman who would remove the blemish. All suggestions were unacceptable to the king, for none could repair the imperfection.

Some time lapsed and a wise, imaginative jeweler examined the blemished jewel. He told the king he had an ingenious idea to restore the ruby to greater elegance and beauty.

"Such a magnificent gem ought to bear the coat of arms of Your Highness. This scratch will be a perfect beginning for the design. From here I will continue to engrave the full coat of arms."

This jeweler transformed the imperfection into a design of perfection and beauty.

—Dubno Maggid

3. *As the fool walks on the road he lacks proper sense and proclaims to all that he is a fool.*

Proclaims to all that he is a fool.

Once a donkey found a lion's skin. He put it on and started walking. He noticed that whoever, man or animal, saw him ran away. At first he was rather proud that he became so important that other creatures feared and respected him.

It made him happy that he had the good sense to dress up in the lion's skin. Delighted to have reached such status, he lifted up his loud and harsh voice and began to bray.

Now everybody recognized that it was a donkey. His owner rushed up to him, punishing him for the fright he had created, and said to the donkey, "I recognized you by your voice."

—Mishlay Shu'olim

4. *If the temper of the ruler is aroused against you, do not resign your post, for mildness appeases great offenses.*

Mildness appeases great offenses.

Rabbi Simon said: "Be ever gentle as a reed and never rigid as a cedar." A reed, even though the winds of the world blow, bends with the wind and straightens out with it. When the winds subside the reed remains in its place. In the end, the reed is worthy to be the pen that writes the secrets of the Torah. But not so with the cedar. If a wind blows from the northwest, the cedar is torn down. If the wind blows from the southwest it blows down the cedar, uproots and throws it down in its place. This is the way you will find it. And the end of this cedar is that people come and chop it up and what is left they throw into the fire. That is why, "Be ever gentle as a reed and never rigid as a cedar!"

—Derech Eretz Rabbah

5. *There is an evil which I observed under the sun that is like an error committed by a despot.*

Like an error committed by a despot.

The government of Rome issued a decree that Jews were forbidden to study the Torah or circumcise their sons and that they must work on the Sabbath. What did Judah ben Shamua and his colleagues do? They went to seek advice from a prominent matron whom all Roman nobility used to visit. Her advice was, "Go and make demonstrations at night time."
They went and demonstrated at night and proclaimed,

"O, in Heaven's name, are we not your brothers? Are we not the sons of one father? Are we not the sons of one mother? Why are we different from every nation and people that you make such severe decrees against us?"

The decrees were withdrawn and that day was proclaimed a feast day.

—Talmud, Rosh Hashana p. 19a

6. *Folly is placed in high positions while the noble sit in low places.*

While the noble sit in low places.

Rabbi Joseph, son of Rabbi Joshua was sick and fell into a trance. After he recovered his father asked him, "What did you see?"

"I saw there in heaven the world upside down, the upper class below and the lower class on top."

"My son," commented the father, "you have seen a clear world."

—Talmud, Pesochim p. 50a

7. *I have seen slaves upon horses while princes were walking on the ground like slaves.*

Slaves upon horses.

The tail of a snake protested to its head, "How long will you continue to lead while I drag behind. Let me lead."

The head agreed and said, "Go first."

The tail started to lead and immediately got into a path of thorns. The tail got deeper into the thorns dragging the head behind.

They came to a pit filled with water and fell into the pit. They approached a fire. Instead of avoiding it, the tail dragged them into the fire.

Who was to blame? The head was blame-worthy, because it allowed the tail to lead. This is what happens when the leaders follow instead of leading. All are hurt.

—Midrash Rabbah Dvorim I

8. *He who digs a pit will fall into it and he who breaks down a fence will be bitten by a snake.*

Hillel saw a skull floating on the surface of the water. He said to it, "Because you drowned others they have drowned you. In the end they who drowned you will be drowned."

—Talmud, Sukah p. 53a
Ethics of the Fathers 2:7

The Midrash has applied this to two historical episodes.

In Egypt, King Pharaoh charged the midwives, "Every son that is born to the Israelites shall ye cast into the river." (Exodus 1:22) By the same means, water, God overthrew Pharaoh and his hosts. They were drowned in the Red Sea.

Haman sought to annihilate the Jews in Persia. He made gallows upon which to hang Mordecai, as told in the Book of Esther. In the end, "The King commanded by letters that the wicked scheme which he (Haman) had devised against the Jews shall come upon his own head and that he and his sons should be hanged on the gallows." (Esther 9:25)

—Midrash Rabbah, Ecclesiastes 10:8

9. *He who removes stones may be hurt by them; he who splits logs may be harmed by them.*

He who removes stones may be hurt by them.

The rule is that one should not remove stones from his own property to public ground. It happened that a man was engaged in doing precisely this when a pious man passed by.

The pious man said to him, "Foolish man, why do you

remove stones from property not belonging to you unto your own property?"

The man laughed at this absurd remark. At a later date this man was compelled to sell his land. Walking on the public highway in front of his former land he stumbled over the very stones he once had thrown there. Then he exclaimed, "Oh, how right was that pious man when he warned me not to move the stones."

—Talmud, Baba Kamma p. 50b

10. *If an ax is dull and one does not sharpen its edge, one must exert more strength. There is an advantage in wise preparation.*

There is an advantage in wise preparation.

A simple young man from a small village visited a large city. At night he was awakened from his sleep by the loud and strange noise of a screeching whistle.

"What does this mean?" he asked in fright. He was told that a fire had broken out and that the screeching whistle was the city's fire alarm. He dressed quickly and he saw a man standing on a high tower, blowing the whistle until he was told the fire had been extinguished.

The simple stranger was so impressed with this marvelous instrument that could put out a fire that the next day he bought such a shrill whistle to take home.

At home in the village he told the people about his magical invention. From then on he would be responsible for putting out any fire.

Sometime later a fire broke out. The young man went into the main street and started blowing a fire alarm whistle, producing a frightful, screeching noise. In the meantime half the houses in the village had gone up in flames.

Angered and frustrated he returned to the city and told the seller of the whistle, "You are a fraud. There was a fire in our village. I blew the whistle but it did not put out the fire."

"Why, you fool," said the merchant, "the whistle is intended to call out the fire brigade to fight the fire and put it out. If you have not prepared a fire brigade, the whistle won't put out any fire."

—Dubno Maggid

11. *If a serpent bites before being charmed what is the use of having a trained charmer?*

What is the use of having a trained charmer?

Three scientists decided to pool their skills. One invented a wonderful telescope. The second invented a flying vehicle. The third, a miracle drug.

The inventor of the telescope reported to his two friends that he had observed the king's palace far away and the princess was desperately ill. All three got into the flying vehicle which brought them to the king's palace.

The third scholar then treated the princess with his miraculous drug and she instantly showed signs of recovery.

Then the king proclaimed that the princess would marry the man who had saved her life.

Each of the three claimed that his particular contribution was primarily instrumental in saving her life.

The choice was finally given to the princess. She said that each had a share in her recovery but she would choose to marry the inventor of the drug. "Neither seeing everything nor travelling anywhere is as important to me as my good health."

—Dubno Maggid

12. *Words from the mouth of a wise man gain favor but the lips of a fool destroy him.*

181

> Words from the mouth of a wise man gain favor.
> The wise man speaks and teaches so that his words will
> be effective and acceptable.
>
> —Rashi

Rabbi Preido had a pupil. Whatever he taught he would repeat 400 times, so that the pupil could master it.

One day the Rabbi was invited to attend a religious service. He taught as usual but the pupil did not learn the lesson. "Why is today different?" asked the Rabbi.

The pupil replied, "From the time the Master was invited to attend that religious service, I have been unable to concentrate my thoughts. Every minute I said to myself, now the Master is going to leave, now the Master is going to leave."

"Now pay attention to your lesson. I will repeat the lesson." He taught him another four hundred times.

—Talmud, Eruvin p. 54b

13. *The beginning of his speech is foolishness and the end of his speech is mischievous madness.*

The end of his speech is mischievous madness.

A great king had an only son who was stupid. As this prince became older, the king sought in every way to provide a little more training, a little more knowledge, a little more education, but with no improvement. The king and his ministers decided to send the prince to a university in a distant land. The king was promised that there special teachers would be able to help his son.

The prince left for the university and remained for ten years. Then he wrote his father that he had learned much. He had studied history, geography, astronomy, mathematics and science. It was decided that the prince return.

A reception was arranged to welcome him back. Among the guests was one of his old teachers who wanted to see the great change in his former pupil.

The teacher asked him about his studies. Then the teacher took off a ring from his finger and kept it in the palm of his hand. He asked the prince, "Since you are so wise, tell me what I have in the palm of my hand."

The prince thought a moment and said, "According to the logic of engineering I would say that you have in your hand a round object with a hole in it."

The teacher gasped at this remarkable and nearly accurate answer. In this spirit the teacher said, "Can your Highness tell us just exactly what this round object is?"

The prince replied, "According to the logic of my studies, I have nothing to add, but according to my own reason I would imagine it is the wheel of a truck."

—Dubno Maggid

14. *A fool multiplies words. Man does not know what is about to be. Who can tell him what will happen after that.*

A fool multiplies words.

A farmer had a parrot. The parrot could only say the words, "There is no doubt about it." This was all it could learn. All day long it would whistle a tune or cry out, "There is no doubt about it." To every question the parrot gave the same reply.

One day the farmer went to the market to sell the parrot. "Who will buy my parrot for twenty dollars," the farmer announced.

A man hearing the high price turned to the parrot and asked, "Are you worth twenty dollars?"

"There is no doubt about it," was the parrot's reply.

The man was so pleased with the bird's reply that he bought it and carried it home.

Some time later he regretted the purchase. Standing beside the cage of the parrot the new owner said, "Twenty dollars was too much. What a fool I was to throw so much money away.

"There is no doubt about it, there is no doubt about it," cried the bird.

—Mishlay Shu'olim

15. *The efforts of the fool exhaust him so that he does not know his way to the city.*

The sense of the verse is that the fool is so brainless that he cannot follow the well-marked open road to the city.

A fox wandered into the storeroom of a theatre. As he looked around the room he saw a face with a stern appearance glaring down at him. He became frightened. Since the face did not move from its place, he waited a while. Then he approached it to find that is was only a mask that actors use. "Ah," said the fox, "you look like the head of a man, but you have no brain."

—Harvard Classics

16. *Woe to you, O land, when your king is a youth and your princes feast in the morning.*

This sentence is reflected in a crucial event in Jewish history following the death of King Solomon.

Then Solomon slept with his fathers and was buried in the City of David, his father and Rehoboam his son reigned in his stead. They (the people) spoke to Rehoboam, saying, "Your father made our yoke heavy. Now then lighten the grievous service of your father and his heavy yoke which he laid upon us and we will serve you."

Then he said to them, "Go away for three days, then return to me." So the people went away. Then King Rehoboam took counsel with the old men who had stood before Solomon his father, while he was still alive, saying, "How do you advise me to reply to this people?"

They spoke to him saying, "If you will be a servant to this people today and will serve them, and when you answer, speak kindly to them, then they will be your servants forever."

But he rejected the counsel of the old men and took counsel with the young men, who had grown up with him and who were his companions. He said to them, "What do you advise that we reply to this people, who have spoken to me saying, "Lighten the yoke that your father laid upon us."

Then the young men who had grown up with him spoke to him saying, "Thus shall you say to this people who spoke to you, 'My little finger is thicker than my father's loins. And now, whereas my father loaded you with a heavy yoke, I will add to your yoke; my father chastised you with a heavy yoke, I will add to your yoke; my father chastised you with whips, but I will chastise you with scorpions.'

So when Jeroboam and all the people came to Rehoboam on the third day, the king answered them harshly and rejected the counsel of the old men. And he spoke to them according to the counsel of the young men saying, "My father made your yoke heavy, but I will add to your yoke; my father chastised you with whips, but I will chastise you with scorpions."

Now when all Israel saw that the king had not listened to them, the people replied to the king saying, "What portion have we in David? Yea, we have no heritage in the son of Jesse. To your tents, O Israel." (This rebellion led to the division of the Jewish Kingdom.)

—I Kings 12:1-17

17. *Happy are you, O land, when your king is a free man and your princes feast at the proper time, with restraint and not in drunkenness.*

When your king is a free man.

Two women of ill fame came to the king (Solomon) and stood before him. One woman said, "O, my lord, this woman and I dwell in the same house and I gave birth to a child while she was in the house. Then on the third day after I was delivered, this woman also gave birth to a child and we were together, there being no stranger with us in the house besides us two.

"But the child of this woman died in the night, because she lay upon it. Then she arose in the middle of the night and took my son from my side while your maid-servant slept and laid it in her bosom and laid her dead child in my bosom. Thus when I arose in the morning to nurse my child, behold, it was dead. But when I was able to examine it closely in the morning, behold, it was not my son whom I had borne."

"No, but the living child is mine and the dead child is your child," the other woman said. But the first woman said, "No, but the living child is mine and the dead child is your child."

Thus they spoke before the king. Then the king said, "This one declares, 'This is my child, the living one, and your child is dead.' And the other declares, 'No, but your son is the dead and my son is the living.'

"Get me a sword," said the king. So they brought in a sword before the king. The king then said, "Cut the living child in two and give half to one and half to the other."

But the woman to whom the living child belonged spoke to the king, for her motherly tenderness was aroused for her son and she said, "O my lord, give her the living child and by no means slay it."

But the other interrupted, "It shall be neither mine or yours. Divide it!"

Then the king answered and said, "Give her the living child and by no means slay it, for she is the mother."

Now when all Israel heard of the judgment that the king had rendered, they stood in awe of the king for they saw that the wisdom of God was in him to administer justice.

—I Kings 3:16-28

18. *Through idleness the roof sinks and through laziness the house becomes flooded.*

Through laziness the house becomes flooded.

The Talmud discusses all sorts of housework a wife must perform in her home. Rabbi Eliezer said, "Even if the wife brought to the husband a hundred servants he may compel her to work in wool for idleness leads to immorality."

Rabbi Simon suggests that idleness to a woman is not a moral, but a mental hazard. Rabbi Shimon ben Gamliel said, "Idleness leads to dullness."

—Talmud, Kethuboth p. 59b

19. *A feast is made for levity and wine to cheer life and money answers it all.*

Money answers it all.

In his march to conquer the ancient world, Alexander of Macedonia travelled to distant and remote countries. When he reached the land of Katzio, he said to the king, "I came here to discover your laws and customs."

One day two citizens came before the king that he might judge their dispute. The plaintiff first presented his case. "I bought a piece of land from this man and I found on it a treasure. I bought land and not a treasure. The money then is not mine."

The seller argued, "I sold him the land and all it contained. The treasure really belongs to him."

The king as judge asked the seller, "You have a son?" The answer was, "Yes." Then he turned to the buyer, "You have a daughter?" The answer was also, "Yes." "Well then," said the judge to them, "let your son marry your daughter and give the fortune to the young couple."

At this Alexander of Macedonia showed signs of bewilderment. "You think my sentence unfair," asked the king.

"No," said Alexander.

"How would you have handled such a case in your country?" asked the king.

He answered, "We would have executed both and seized the treasure and money from both parties."

Outraged at such greed for money, the king of Katzio asked of Alexander, "Does it rain in your country?"

"Of course," was the answer.

"Does the sun shine in your country?"

"Of course," was again the answer.

"Are there any domestic animals in your country?"

"Yes!"

"The reason there is rain and sunshine in your country is not on account of the people. They would not deserve it. Rain and sunshine continue for the sake of your animals.

—Midrash Rabbah, Genesis 33

20. *Do not curse the king even in your thoughts, nor curse a rich man in your chamber, for a bird in the air may carry the report, and a winged creature relate the matter.*

A bird in the air may carry the report.

Herod was a slave to the royal house of Hasmoneans. He had set his eye on marrying one of this family. One day he heard a voice saying that a slave who would rebel that day would succeed. He then assassinated all the royal family except one princess.

When she discovered that he planned to marry her, she went up on the roof, threw herself down and killed herself.

Herod thought, it is the Rabbis who teach, "From the midst of your brothers shall you set up a king." He therefore killed all the Rabbis except Rabbi Bobo ben Butto with whom he planned to take counsel. Even then he put out his eyes to make him blind.

One day Herod came to visit Rabbi Bobo. Herod said, "Master, do you realize what this wicked slave (Herod) has done?"

"What do you want me to do to him," said the Rabbi.

His answer was, "I want you to curse him."

The Rabbi replied, "It is written that even in your thoughts you must not curse a king."

Herod said to him, "But this is no king."

The Rabbi said, "Even if he be only a rich man, as there is a verse: 'And in your chamber do not curse the rich' and even if he be only a prince, it is written: 'A prince among your people you shall not curse.'"

Herod then said, "This can only apply to one who acts as one of your people."

The Rabbi said, "I am afraid of him."

Herod responded, "But there is no one who can tell since we two are alone."

The Rabbi replied with a verse: " 'For a bird in the air may carry the report and a winged creature will relate the matter.'"

Herod then said, "I am Herod. Had I known that the Rabbis were so wise, I should not have killed them."

—Talmud, Baba Bathra p. 3b

CHAPTER ELEVEN

1. *Cast your bread upon the waters, for after many days you will find it.*

Cast your bread upon the waters.

While Rabbi Akiva was travelling by sea, he was in a shipwreck. He was worried about a Rabbinical sage who went down with the ship. When he arrived at the port of Coppodolia, he found the sage talking to the people. Rabbi Akiva asked him, "My son, how were you saved from the sea?"

He replied, "It must have been your prayer on my behalf. Wave after wave came and pushed me ashore."

Rabbi Akiva asked, "My son, what good have you done that you were saved from drowning?"

He answered, "Before boarding ship, a poor man met me and pleaded, 'Help me.' I gave him one loaf of bread. In thanking me he said, 'As you have saved my life by your gift so may your life be saved.'"

Rabbi Akiva then applied to him, "Cast your bread upon the waters."

—Midrash Rabbah, Ecclesiastes 11:1

2. *Give a portion to seven and even to eight, for you never know what misfortune will happen in the land.*

Give a portion to seven and even to eight.

Eliezer of Bartotha was an extremely charitable man. When the collectors of charity would see him, they would hide themselves from him for he was in the habit of giving away all he had. One day he was going out to buy a trousseau for his daughter. The collectors of charity saw him and they hid from him. He ran after them and said, "I beg you to tell me for what cause you are collecting?"

They told him, "It is for an orphaned bride and an orphaned bridegroom."

"I swear that they deserve priority over the needs of my daughter."

He then took all the money he had and gave it to them. He left himself one zuz (small silver coin). With this zuz he bought wheat which he took home and put in his corn bin.

When his wife came home she asked the daughter, "What did your father bring home?"

She answered, "Whatever father brought home he put into the corn bin."

The wife went to the corn bin and tried to open the door but it was so full of wheat that she could not open the door.

The daughter ran to the House of Study to tell her father. "Come home and see what your friend (God) has done for you."

He then pledged that all the grain be devoted to a sacred cause and that his daughter derive no more from this miracle than any other poor person.

—Talmud, Taanith p. 24a

3. *If the clouds be filled with rain they empty out on the earth; if a tree falls southward or northward, where the tree falls there it will remain.*

The author cites two illustrations, rain and windstorm whose causes are beyond man's power to comprehend or control.

Rabbi Z'eira found Rabbi Judah standing by the door of his father-in-law's house. He noticed that Rabbi Judah was in a cheerful mood and he thought to himself, "Now if I were to ask him all the secrets of the universe he would tell me."

He asked, "Why do goats march ahead of the flock and then the sheep?"

Rabbi Judah answered, "This is as it was at the time of creation, darkness preceded light."

"Why are sheep covered (with fat tails) while goats are uncovered (with thin tails)?"

"Those whose materials will cover us are themselves covered while those who do not give us goods to cover us, are uncovered."

"Why is the tail of a camel short?"

"Because it eats thorns (a long tail would tangle in the thorns)."

"Why is the tail of an ox long?"

"Because it feeds in meadows and chases away the gnats."

"Why is the facial part of a locust flexible?"

"Because it lives among willows and if it were hard, the upper part might be injured and it would go blind."

"Why is the lower eyelid of fowl bent upward?"

"Because it lives among rafters and if dust entered into its eye, it would go blind."

—Talmud, Sabbath p. 77b

4. *A wind watcher will never sow, and a cloud gazer will never reap.*

There is need for action in life. In this story two handicapped boys applied themselves to study and succeeded.

There were two deaf and dumb boys in the neighborhood of Rabbi Judah the Prince. They were the sons of the daughter of Rabbi Yochanan ben Godguda. When Rabbi Judah went into the academy of learning they would follow him. They sat down, shook their heads and moved their lips.

Rabbi Judah prayed for them and they were healed. It was found that they were well versed in Halacha (laws) and the entire six sections of the Mishna and Talmud.

—Talmud, Chagiga p. 3a

5. *As you do not know the course of the wind nor what is the embryo in a pregnant womb, so you cannot know the actions of God who has created all.*

There are mysteries in nature, as well as in man, which we see and do not understand. It is so, too, with God's rule of the universe. In the following story, at the end of levels of reason Moses substitutes faith.

We learn in the Talmud (Rosh Hashana 21) that forty-nine out of fifty levels of reason were given to Moses. But since man yearns to know more, how did Moses continue to study? The answer is that when he found the fiftieth level too complex and unapproachable by the human mind, he substituted faith and meditated further upon those aspects of knowledge open to him.

In this way everybody ought to discipline his mind. He should study and reflect to the utmost of his ability. When he has reached a point where he is unable to comprehend further, he may substitute faith, then returning to the learning that is within his grasp. Beyond a certain degree of understanding, both the wise and the ignorant are alike.

—Baal Shem Tov, Tifereth Yehudah

6. *In the morning sow your seed and in the evening let not your hand rest for you never know which will excel, one or the other, or if both may turn out equally well.*

In the morning sow your seed.

There was a man who lost all his wealth, but he had a devoted wife. He was so poor he had to work in the field for hire.

Elijah the Prophet came and told him, "You shall have seven prosperous years. When do you want them, now or in your old age?" Elijah spoke to him on three different occasions. Finally the man replied, "I will go home and consult my wife.

He went home and told his wife that someone had come to him three times and told him, "You shall have seven good years. When do you want them, now or in your old age?"

She replied, "Tell him we want them now."

The man returned and told Elijah that he wanted them then and not later.

He was told to go home and "when you reach your house your blessing will be there."

At that same time his children were playing in the dirt and found a fortune. They called their mother and when the father reached the house, the mother told him what happened. They both thanked God for this kindness.

What did this good and pious woman do? She said to her husband, "God has been merciful and granted us this gift of seven prosperous years. Let us practice kindness and give charity to the poor out of our money during the seven years. Perhaps God will increase our good fortune." She told her youngest son to keep a record of her charity.

At the end of seven years Elijah appeared to the man and told him the time had come "to take what I have given to you."

The man replied: "When I accepted your offer I consult-

195

ed my wife. I cannot therefore return this without my wife's consent."

The husband told his wife that the old man had come and wanted back all the money that was given to them.

She told her husband: "Go and say to the man, 'If you can find people more trustworthy than we are, I will return to you all the money.' "

God heard their words and saw the acts of charity they had performed. Instead of taking it away, he added greater prosperity.

—Midrash Zuta, Ruth 4:11

7. *Sweet is the light and pleasant for the eyes to see the sunshine.*

Sweet is the light.

Rabbi Simloey said, "What is meant by the verse: 'Woe unto you that desire the day of the Lord.' What good is it to you? The day of the Lord is darkness and not light." (Amos 5:18)

The Prophet was addressing the wicked nations. This may be compared to a rooster and a bat who were hopefully waiting for the light of dawn. The rooster said to the bat, "I look forward to the light because I have sight, but of what use is the light to you?"

—Talmud, Sanhedrin p. 98b

8. *Though a man live many years let him be happy in all of them and let him remember that the days of darkness will be many; all that is coming is futility.*

The days of darkness.

Samuel said to Rabbi Yehudah: "Shinena (clever one), hurry on and eat, hurry and drink (do not postpone any enjoyment of life), since the world from which we must depart is like a wedding feast." (Its enjoyment is short and ends abruptly.)

Rav said to Rabbi Hamnuna: "My son, do good to yourself according to your ability for there is no enjoyment in the grave, nor will death be long in coming. And should you say, "I will leave my wealth to my children, who will tell you in the grave?' " (That it is being put to good use.)

—Talmud, Eruvin p. 54a

9. *Be happy, young man, in your youth and let your heart cheer you in the days of your manhood; follow the inclinations of your heart and the sight of your eyes; but know that for all this God will bring you to account.*

Be happy, young man, in your youth.

Rabbi Samuel ben Rabbi Yitzchok said: "The Rabbis sought to suppress the Book of Ecclesiastes. They found in this book thoughts that contained heretical tendencies. They objected asking, 'Is this the wisdom of Solomon, to say, "Be happy, young man, in your youth?" ' "

Had not Moses warned: "Go not after your own heart." (Numbers 15:39)

Yet Solomon now says: "Follow the inclinations of your heart." Is restraint to be abolished? Is there no judgment and no judge?

But since Solomon concluded: "But know that for all this God will bring you into account," the Rabbis exclaimed: "Well had Solomon spoken."

—Midrash Rabbah, Ecclesiastes 11:9

10. *Banish anger from your heart and avoid abuse of your body; for youth and manhood are fleeting.*

Banish anger from your heart.

A man should ever be as meek as Hillel and not as prone to anger as Shammai.

Once, two men made a bet with each other, that the one who would make Hillel angry would win four hundred zuz.

One offered: "I will go and cause him anger." On Friday Hillel was washing his hair. This man came to the front of Hillel's house and shouted rudely, "Where is Hillel, where is Hillel?" (intending to be discourteous)

Hillel put on his mantle and went out to meet him saying, "My son, what do you wish?"

The man said, "I want to ask you a question."

Hillel said, "Ask, my son."

"Why are the heads of Babylonians round?"

"You have asked a very good question; because their midwives lack proper skill."

The man left and waited one hour. He returned and shouted again, "Where is Hillel, where is Hillel?"

Again Hillel dressed and went out to see him and said, "What is it, my son?"

"I would like to ask you a question."

"Ask, my son," was the answer.

"Why are the people of Palmera bleary-eyed?"

Hillel replied, "You have asked a very good question, because they live in sandy country."

The man left and returned later and shouted, "Where is Hillel, where is Hillel?"

Hillel put on his garments, went out to see him and asked, "What do you wish?"

"I want to ask you a question."

"Ask, my son, ask."

The man asked, "Why are the feet of the Africans wide?"

"My son, you have asked a good question; because they live near swamps."

Then the man said, "I have many more questions to ask, but I am afraid that you will get angry."

Hillel then sat down with him and said, "You can ask me all the questions you want to ask."

"Are you the Hillel who is called a prince in Israel." (Head of a College)

"Yes," he answered.

"If that is so, may there not be many like you in Israel?"

"Why, my son?" asked Hillel.

"Because you have caused me to lose four hundred silver coins," the man complained.

Hillel said to him, "Be careful of your whims. For better that you should lose four hundred zuzim and another four hundred zuzim, yet Hillel should not lose his temper."

—Talmud, Sabbath p. 30b

CHAPTER TWELVE

1. *Remember your Creator in the days of your vigor before the days of trouble come and the years are reached when you will say, "I have no pleasure in them."*

Remember your Creator in the days of your vigor.

Rabbi Zalman Chasid was on his death bed. His friends came to his bedside and asked him to recite the confession. The Rabbi said, "Do you really believe a death bed confession is very important? Not at all. It is not important for a man to make confession on his death bed when he is powerless to do anything else. A confession should be made when a man is in full vigor seated at his dining table, when he can still eat, drink, and act."

—Shivchay Tzadikim p. 32

2. *Before the sun and the light and the moon and the stars grow dark and the clouds return after the rain.*

This, and the four following sentences are a poetic description of the oncoming of old age. This describes the impaired vision and sight clouded with tears as a result of pain and illness.

Until the time of Abraham there was no old age. (Old age did not mark a person.) Whoever wished to speak to Abraham would mistakenly speak to his son Isaac. Whoever wished to speak to Isaac might unwittingly speak to Abraham. Then Abraham prayed and old age came into existense. As is it written, "And Abraham was old and well advanced in age." (Genesis 24:1)

—Talmud, Baba Metzia p. 87a

3. *In the day when the guards of the house become shaky and the strong men will stoop, and the grinders cease because they are few and those that look out the windows are dimmed.*

This sentence portrays the loss of vigor, loss of teeth and of vision.

The Talmud tells in this regard that, until the time of Jacob, there was no sickness (death occurred suddenly). Then Jacob prayed and illness came into existence. As it is said, "Behold your father is sick." (Genesis 42:1)

—Talmud, Baba Metzia p. 87a

4. *The doors to the street are shut, as the sound of the mill is low and one wakes at the song of a bird and all the strains of music are hushed.*

In this sentence the reference is to the failing of digestion, insomnia and the loss of hearing.

The emperor asked Rabbi Joshua ben Chanania: "Why did you not attend the Be-Abedan (place of heathen religious discussions)?"

He answered, "The mountain (my head) is snowy and surrounded by ice (my beard). The dog (my voice) does not bark and the grinders (my teeth) do not grind."

In the School of Rav they used to say (as a description of old age), "What I did not lose I seek." (An old man walks bent and stooping.)

—Talmud, Sabbath p. 152a

5. *They are afraid of every height and of the terrors on the road; and the almond tree blossoms and the grasshopper is a burden and the caperberry is impotent; because man goes to his eternal home and the mourners go about in the street.*

Here he speaks of nervousness, walking with unsteady tread, the graying of the hair, the inability to care for oneself, and the decline of all desire.

Rabbi Shimon ben Chalafta used to visit Rabbi Yehudah Hanassi each month. As he got old he was unable to do this. On one occasion he did repeat his visit. The host said to him, "Why have I proved worthy to see you today?"

The guest replied, "Distant objects have become near and near objects have become distant; two has become three and what used to bring peace has ceased."

The explanation of his remark is this: "Distant objects have become near . . ." (The eyes which used to see from a distance cannot now see even that which is near.) "Near objects seem far . . ." (The ears which used to hear after the first or second comment cannot hear after a hundred repetitions.) "Two have become three . . ." (I have a stick in addition to my two legs.) "What used to bring peace in the house has ceased . . ." (Sexual desire between man and wife.)

—Midrash Rabbah, Ecclesiastes 12:5

6. *Before the silver cord is parted and the golden bowl is shattered and the pitcher is broken at the fountain and the wheel is smashed into the well.*

Here the description is of the dissolution of the bodily organs including the spinal cord, the skull and the stomach.

At the time when a child is formed in its mother's womb there are three partners, God, the father, and the mother.

At the time of death, God takes the portion which he provided and leaves those parts provided by the father and mother.

They weep. God says to them: "Why do you weep? Have I taken away anything of yours? I have taken only that which is mine."

They say: "Lord of the universe, as long as your portion was part of ours, our portion was protected from worms and insects. Now you have taken away your part from our parts, our part is unprotected."

Rabbi Yehudah Hanassi used to tell a parable. "This is to be likened to a king who rented his orchard to a tenant. The king later ordered his servants, 'Go cut down the grapes of my orchard and bring my portion and leave there the portion which belongs to my tenant.'

"The servants did as he commanded. The tenant complained and cried. The king said to him, 'Have I taken any of your fruit? I have only taken my part.' The tenant replied: 'My Lord, as long as your portion mingled with mine, my portion was protected from robbery and theft. Now that you have taken away your portion, my portion is exposed to robbery and theft.'"

The King is the Supreme King of Kings, God; the tenant is the father and mother. As long as the soul is within the human being he is protected, but when he dies he is exposed to all elements.

—Midrash Rabbah, Ecclesiastes 5:10

7. *And the dust returns to the earth as it was and the spirit returns to God Who gave it.*

This sentence is similar to the description in Genesis 2:7. "The Lord God formed man from the dust of the earth and breathed into his nostrils the breath of life and man became a living being." Following a description of the deterioration and disintegration of man, the author differentiates between the earthly and spiritual aspects of man.

The story is related that Bezalel, the chief architect of the Israelites' tabernacle in the wilderness, became desperately ill at the conclusion of its building. Moses came to see him and Bezalel requested that Moses offer a prayer for his health.

As a response, Moses asked Bezalel how he went about constructing the tabernacle of the Lord.

In his weak and sick condition he slowly answered, "As well as I can remember, when the charge came to me, I knew I would need gold, silver, metal and even wood which is rare in the wilderness. Instead of seeking these materials, I first took sand and built a model of the entire tabernacle. From this pattern of sand I calculated what materials I would need and then asked for them. As a matter of fact, that is how I went about making all the holy vessels. I made a model of sand for the Holy Ark and then procured the material. I made a model of sand for the altar as well as the Menorah and then I ordered the material."

Moses then said, "I know you are weak. I have only one more question to ask you. What did you do with the models of sand after you had built the real objects?"

Bezalel smiled and said: "Of what possible use were the models after I had the real things?

Then Moses said: "You are a human architect. This is just what the Divine Architect does. God wants to create a human soul. But the soul too needs a model of sand, the body of man. Until the soul has achieved its mission and fulfilled its purpose it has need of the model of sand. Once the soul has been built and fulfilled, the model of sand is no longer of any use.

—Oral Tradition

8. *Vanity of vanities, says Koheleth, all is illusion.*

All is illusion.

When the rays of the sun enter a house through a dusty window they form illumined pillars. If one attempts to feel them, he discovered there is nothing there. Worldly desires are comparable to these seeming pillars fashioned by the sun.

—Tifereth Hatzadikim

9. *In addition to Koheleth having been a wise man he also taught the people knowledge. Pondering and searching, he composed many parables.*

He composed many parables.

Do not underestimate the value of a parable for through it man acquired the foundation for learning Torah. If one loses a great treasure of pearls, one uses in searching for these valued objects, a candle, which in itself is of little value.

In search for the treasures of Torah the place of the candle is taken by the parable. A parable alone has no worth. Its only value is when it is used as a light, to illumine the mystery and to explain the inscrutable parts.

You can buy a candle for a penny and when put to its proper use, it can become most profitable. Similarly, the parable may be very simple, but put in its proper place it can achieve miracles. The more simple and direct the parable, the more successful will be its application.

—Midrash Rabbah, Song of Songs 1:1

10. *Koheleth tried to find acceptable subjects and that which is properly written, words of truth.*

Properly written, words of truth.

He pondered the words of Torah and searched for the meaning of the words of Torah. He created handles to the Torah. You will find that until Solomon there was no parable.

Rabbi Nachman gave two illustrations. Imagine there was a large palace with many entrances and partitions so that who ever entered could not find his way back to the door. Then one clever person came, took a coil of string and fastened it to the door, so that all could come in and out by following the coil.

So, until Solomon no one was able to properly understand the words of the Torah. As soon as Solomon came, all began to comprehend the Torah.

Rabbi Nachman gave another illustration of a thicket of reeds which no one could penetrate. One clever man came and took a scythe and cut some down. Then all began to enter through that opening. This did Solomon do for the study of Torah.

Rabbi Yossi said, "Imagine a big basket full of produce, without any handles, so that it could not be lifted. Then one clever man came and made handles for it and from that time on it was carried by the handles. So until Solomon came, no one could properly understand the words of the Torah, but when Solomon came, all began to comprehend the Torah."

—Midrash Rabbah, Song of Songs 1:1

11. *The words of the wise are like goads and like well fastened nails are the words of the masters of assemblies. They were given by one Shepherd.*

They were given by one Shepherd.

Once a heathen came to Shammai and asked him, "How many Torahs (systems of law) have you?"

He answered, "We have two, the Written Law and the Oral Law."

"I believe you in regards to the Written Law, but not the Oral Law. Now accept me as a proselyte on condition that you teach me the Written Law (only)."

Shammai angrily drove him away.

The heathen then went to Hillel who accepted him as a proselyte. On the first day he instructed him aleph, beth, gimmel, daleth (the first letters of the alphabet). The next day he reversed the letters in teaching him.

The man protested saying, "Yesterday you taught me the opposite order."

Hillel answered, "You see that you must rely upon me as to which is correct. Then you ought to rely upon me with regards to the entire Oral Torah, too." (There must be reliance upon authority. The text of the Written Law is only comprehensible together with the oral tradition.)

—Talmud, Sabbath p. 31a

12. *Of more than these be warned, my son, of making many books there is no end and excessive studying is physically exhausting.*

The warning here is against too many books. This causes confusion, exhaustion and waste of energy. The author directs the reader to one source of wisdom, "the words of the wise," which will bring inspiration and discipline. It is true there are varied sources of wisdom. At best, these lead to physical weariness.

In this verse the Hebrew text contains the word "mehema" (these). The Midrash says, "Read this word as 'mehuma' (confusion), because whoever brings into his house more than the 24 books of the Bible introduces confusion into his house."

—Midrash Rabbah, Ecclesiastes 12:12

Rova preached the following on the meaning of the verse, "Of more than these be warned, my son, of making many books there is no end": Be more careful in the observance of the words of the Scribes than the words of the Torah. In case you will ask, "If they are of real value, why were they not recorded in the Torah?" The answer is found in our Scriptural statement "of making many books there is no end."

—Talmud, Eruvin p. 21b

King Ptolemy Philadelphus of Egypt (285-247 B.C.E.) assembled 72 Elders, the wise men of Jerusalem. He had them placed in 72 separate rooms without telling them why he brought them together. He then went to each of them and said to each one, "Translate for me the Torah of Moses, your Master."

—Talmud, Megillah p. 9a

Based on these Talmudical statements a Sephardi Rabbi tells two relevant stories. There was once a great King Ptolemy who succeeded Alexander of Macedonia in ruling Egypt. He had a most extensive library. It contained 995 books. Eager to acquaint himself with world culture he wanted to acquire books from all nations. The King expressed a wish to his counsellors, "If only I could gather five more books, that would complete my happiness."

Others tell of King Ptolemy's large and varied library. His counsellors told him that all the books he had were of no substance in comparison with the books of the Jews in

Jerusalem. They told the King, "If you want to enjoy and enrich yourself, send for some wise men in Jerusalem who know Greek. Let them translate for you the 24 books of the Bible."

The High Priest in Jerusalem honored the King's request and sent 72 wise men who were received with great honor. The King watched and eagerly read each portion of the translation as they progressed. He marvelled at the wisdom of these books.

He said, "I am amazed that up to now no King had thought of translating such books of wisdom."

—Yalkut Me'ahm Loayz p. 37

13. *The sum of the matter, all having been heard, fear God and keep His commandments for this is the whole duty of man.*

Fear God and keep His commandments.

Rabbi Simloey preached that six hundred and thirteen precepts were committed to Moses, three hundred and sixty-five negative commandments, corresponding to the number of days in the solar year (embracing time) and two hundred and forty-eight positive commandments corresponding to the number of organs (bones covered with flesh and sinews), in the human body (embracing man).

King David came and reduced them to eleven. A Psalm of David: Who shall sojourn in your Tabernacle? Who shall dwell on your holy mountain? (1) He who walks uprightly; (2) who does right; (3) speaks truth from his heart; (4) has no slander upon his tongue; (5) does no wrong to his fellow. (6) Nor takes up a reproach against his neighbor; (7) In whose eyes a vile person is despised; (8) he honors those who fear the Lord; (9) he swears to his own hurt and does not retract. (10) He does not put his money on interest; (11) nor takes a bribe against the innocent. (Psalm XV)

Isaiah came and reduced them to six: (1) he who walks uprightly; (2) speaks sincerely; (3) he who despises the gain of oppression; (4) he who keeps his hand free from holding bribes; (5) who stops his ears against hearing of blood shed; (6) who closes his eyes against looking on evil. (Isaiah 33:15-16)

Micah came and reduced them to three. "It has been told you, O Man, what is good and what the Lord requires of you: (1) only to do justice; (2) love mercy; (3) and walk humbly before your God. (Micah 6:8) Again Isaiah came and reduced them to two, "Thus says the Lord: (1) keep you justice; (2) do righteousness. (Isaiah 56:1)

Amos came and reduced them to one principle. "For thus says the Lord to the House of Israel: "Seek Me and you will live." (Amos 4:4)

Rabbi Nachman ben Isaac prefers this conclusion: Habakuk came and based them all on one principle. "But the righteous shall live by his faith." (Habakuk 2:4)

—Talmud, Makkoth p. 23b

14. *For every deed whether good or bad, even those hidden, God will bring into judgment.*

God will bring into judgment.

At the end of their days the poor, the rich, and the sensualist will appear before the heavenly court. The poor man will be asked, "Why didn't you study Torah?" If his reply is, "I was poor and all my time was spent in earning a livelihood," the response of the Court is: "Were you poorer than Hillel?"

Hillel the Elder was a day-laborer who earned one copper coin a day. Half of this money he gave to the guard of the school and the other half he used to provide for himself, his wife, and his children.

One day he earned nothing and the school guard would not let him enter. Hillel climbed up to the roof, lying down on the skylight to hear the words of the living God from the teachers Shmayah and Avtalion. This happened in midwinter, on a Friday, and a heavy snow fell upon him and covered him entirely.

The following morning Shmayah said to Avtalion, "Brother Avtalion, every day at this time the house is light and today it is dark. Is today a cloudy day?"

They looked up to the skylight and saw the figure of a man. They went up to the roof and found Hillel covered by three feet of snow. They carried him down, washed, annointed, and set him near the fire. They said, "This man deserves that the Sabbath may be violated on his account."

The rich man (on the Day of Judgment) is asked: "Why didn't you study Torah?" If his reply is, "I was rich, busy with my possessions," the Court's response is, "Were you richer than Rabbi Eilezar ben Charsum?"

For it is told that Rabbi Eliezer inherited from his father one thousand villages on land and one thousand ships at sea. Nevertheless, every day he would put a bag of flour on his shoulder and go from place to place to study Torah, doing nothing else.

One day his servants, thinking he was a tenant farmer in the village, siezed him to do a day's work. He pleaded with them, "Let me go to study Torah."

They answered, "By the life of our Master, Rabbi Eliezer ben Charsum we shall not let you go free."

He gave them all the money he had, then they let him free. He had never known his servants since he constantly occupied himself with the study of Torah.

A sensual person is asked, "Why didn't you study Torah?" If his reply is, "I was handsome and beset by sensual passions," the Court's response is, "Were you more handsome than Joseph?"

It is related of the saintly Joseph that every day Potiphar's wife tried to tempt him with proposals. The garments she wore in the evening she did not wear in the morning. She said to him, "Yield to me."

He answered, "God releases the imprisoned."

She said, "I will bend your pride" (send you to slave labor).

He answered, "The Lord raises those who are bowed down."

She said, "I will blind your eyes."

He replied, "The Lord opens the eyes of the blind."

She offered him a thousand coins to seduce him, "To lie with her to be near her." (Genesis 39:10)

Joseph would not listen to her.

—Talmud, Yoma p. 35b

SOURCES

CHAPTER ONE

1. *Midrash Rabbah, Song of Songs,* Chapter 1:1
2. *Midrash Rabbah, Ecclesiastes* 1:2
3. *Midrash Rabbah, Ecclesiastes* 5:14
4. Oral Tradition
5. *Talmud, Avoda Zora,* p. 8a
6. *Wisdom of Ben Sira,* 17:26-28
7. *Midrash, Tehillim,* 93
8. *Talmud, Tammid,* p. 32b
9. *Zohar, Vayikra* on 3:1; *Jerusalem Talmud, Avoda Zora* 3:1; *Midrash Rabbah, Bamidbar Nasso* 13; *Talmud, Yoma,* p. 28b
10. *Talmud, Eruvin,* p. 43b; *Tshuvos Yaacov,* David Oppenheimer; *Tossefta Sabbath,* Chapter 7:10
11. Genesis 40:12-14, 21-23; 47:20-25; Exodus 1:6-8
12. *Midrash Rabbah, Ecclesiastes* 1:12
13. *Pirke D'Reb Eliezer* XIII
14. *Midrash Rabbah, Ecclesiastes* 1:14
15. *Midrash Rabbah, Esther* 7
16. *Midrash Rabbah, Ecclesiastes* 1:7
17. Rabbi Yechiel Michal Zlotchover
18. *Talmud, Chagiga,* p. 14b

CHAPTER TWO

1. *Midrash Tanchuma, Noah* 13
2. *Midrash Rabbah, Ecclesiastes* 2:2
3. *Nofess Tzufim,* Pinchoss Koretz
4. I Kings 7:1-13; 9:17-19,24
5. Song of Songs 8:11-19; Talmud, *Yoma,* p. 21b
6. II Chronicles 32:2-4; II Kings 18:17; Isaiah 7:3; 22: 9-11; Nehemiah 3:15,16
7. I Kings 5:2,3,6-8
8. I Kings 10:14-27
9. *Midrash Rabbah, Ecclesiastes* 1:1
10. *Midrash Rabbah, Ecclesiastes* 1-8
11. *Midrash Rabbah, Ecclesiastes* 11:9
12. *Midrash Rabbah, Ecclesiastes* 3:11
13. *Ethics of the Fathers* 6:9
14. *Midrash Rabbah, Ecclesiastes* 9:7
15. Talmud, *Sabbath,* p. 55b
16. *Ohel Yaacov* (Sidrah Achray), Rabbis A. B. Flahm, Yitzchok Kranz
17. Job 3:20-26
18. Jerusalem Talmud, *Sabbath,* Chapter 14:1
19. *Midrash, Lamentations* 1:3
20. *Midrash Rabbah, Ecclesiastes* 2:20
21. Commentary, *Ethics of the Fathers,* Rabbainu Yonah 3:17
22. *Likutay M'haran,* Nathan Nemirov
23. *Ohel Yaacov,* Yissro
24. Talmud, *Sabbath,* p. 119a
25. Talmud, *Pesochim,* p. 86b
26. *Ohel Yaacov,* Toldoth

CHAPTER THREE

1. *Midrash Rabbah, Ecclesiastes* 3:1
2. Talmud, *Sotah,* p. 12a; Talmud, *Sukah,* p. 53a

3. Genesis 6:11-22
4. Talmud, *Makkoth*, p. 24b
5. Ruth 1:8-19
6. *Midrash Rabbah, Ecclesiastes* 3:6
7. Commentary, *Pirke Avoth* 3:17, Rabbi Joseph Nachmies
8. Talmud, *Pesochim*, p. 113b
9. *Ohel Yaacov*, Breishith
10. *Midrash Rabbah, Ecclesiastes* 3:10
11. *Dubno Maggid*, Vol. I, p. 72, Israel J. Zevin
12. Talmud, *Taanith*, p. 22a

13. *Zohs Zichoron*, Yaacov Yitzchock Horowitz
14. Talmud, *Arachin*, p. 10a
15. *Midrash Rabbah, Ecclesiastes* 3:15
16. *Niflo'oth Rabbi Bunam*, Abram Yosef Kleinman
17. *Ethics of the Fathers*, 4:29
18. Chofetz Chaim on *Ethics of the Fathers*, 2:1
19. *Zohar, Bamidbar* Schlach ––––
20. *Yalkut Shimoni* 1:13; *Midrash Shmuel* 31
21. *Yalkut Shimoni* 1:14
22. *Midrash Rabbah, Ecclesiastes* 3:22

CHAPTER FOUR

1. *Mishlay Shu'olim*, Berachia Hanakdon
2. *Midrash Rabbah, Ecclesiastes* 7:1
3. Talmud, *Eruvin*, p. 13b
4. *Mishlay Shu'olim*, Berachia Hanakdon
5. *Midrash Rabbah, Deuteronomy* 8:7
6. *Midrash Rabbah, Ecclesiastes* 4:6
7. *Midrash Rabbah, Genesis* 33
8. Oral Tradition
9. *Midrash Rabbah, Ecclesiastes* 4:9, Adapted from *Yalkut Amos*, p. 549
10. Chief Rabbi Hertz of Great Britain
11. Bar Hebraeus

12. Talmud, *Sanhedrin*, p. 105a
13. *Ben Hamelech Veha'nazir*, Abraham Ibn Chasdai; *Exempla of Rabbis*, Gaster, 390
14. Genesis 41:14-15, 39-45
15. I Kings, 11:26; 40:12-20
16. Talmud, *Sanhedrin*, p. 52b
17. *Midrash Rabbah, Leviticus* 3

CHAPTER FIVE

1. Talmud, *Berochoth*, p. 3a
2. Talmud, *Berochoth*, p. 56a
3. *Midrash Rabbah, Ecclesiastes* 1:1
4. *Yalkut Shimoni*, Matos 784
5. Judges 11:30-40; *Midrash Tanchuma*, Bechukosai 5
6. Talmud, *Brochoth*, p. 28b
7. *Mishlay Shu'olim*, Brachia Hanakdan
8. *Midrash Rabbah, Ecclesiastes* 5:8
9. *Harvard Classics*, Vol. 17, p. 33
10. *Harvard Classics*, Vol. 17, p. 36
11. *Midrash Rabbah, Ecclesiastes* 5:11
12. *Ohel Yaacov*, Vo'esschanon
13. Talmud, *Sabbath*, p. 151b
14. *Midrash Rabbah, Ecclesiastes* 5:14
15. *Ohel Yaacov*, Aykev
16. *Sefer Mussar* 2:13, Rabbi Joseph Ben Judah Ibn Ankin
17. Talmud, *Taanith*, p. 20b
18. Talmud, *Baba Bathra*, p. 11a
19. Talmud, *Berochoth*, p. 30b

CHAPTER SIX

1. *Midrash, Rabbah, Ecclesiastes* 6:1
2. *Dubno Maggid*, Vol. I, p. 43, Israel J. Zevin
3. *Pirke D'Reb Eliezer* XXXIV

4. Job 3:11-16
5. *Midrash Rabbah, Ecclesiastes* 6:5
6. Talmud, *Megillah,* p. 28a
7. *Nofess Tzufim,* Pinchoss Koretz
8. *Kol Yaacov, Koheleth* 1:3, Rabbi Yitzchock Kranz
9. *Mishlay Shu'olim,* Brachia Hanakdan
10. Talmud, *Moed Koton,* p. 18b
11. Dubno Maggid on *Ethics of the Fathers* 6:4
12. *Midrash Rabbah, Ecclesiastes* 1:2

CHAPTER SEVEN

1. Talmud, *Berochoth,* p. 17a; *Midrash Rabbah,* Vayetze, 71
2. Talmud, *Berochoth,* p. 5b
3. *Midrash Rabbah, Ecclesiastes* 7:3
4. *Midrash Rabbah, Ecclesiastes* 9:8
5. Talmud, *Taanith,* p. 20a
6. *Midrash Rabbah, Ecclesiastes* 7:6; *Midrash Rabbah,* Genesis 16
7. Talmud, *Kethuboth,* p. 105b
8. *Tifereth Yehudah,* Baal Shemtov
9. Talmud, *Sabbath,* p. 105b; *Exempla of Rabbis,* Gaster 322
10. Jerusalem Talmud, *Berochoth,* Chapter 1:6
11. Talmud, *Kethoboth,* 103b; *Ethics of Our Fathers* 2:2
12. *Midrash Tanchuma,* Trumah 1:2
13. Talmud, *Taanith,* p. 25a
14. *Midrash Rabbah,* Genesis 27
15. *Midrash Rabbah, Ecclesiastes* 7:15
16. *Midrash Rabbah, Ecclesiastes* 7:16
17. *Ethics of the Fathers* 5:21; I Kings 12:25-33
18. *Midrash Rabbah,* Genesis 9
19. *Midrash Rabbah, Leviticus* 34:16
20. *Exempla of Rabbis,* Gaster 433
21. *Otzar Midrashim,* Eizenstein, Vol. II, p. 327

22. Talmud, *Taanith,* p.7a
23. Talmud, *Sanhedrin,* p. 21b
24. *Likutay M'Haran,* Nathan Nemirov
25. *Nofess Tzufim,* Pinchoss Koretz
26. *Midrash Rabbah, Genesis* 18
27. *Avoth D'Reb Nossan,* Chapter VI
28. *Otzar Midrashim,* Eizenstein, Vol. II, p. 531
29. *Midrash Tanchumah,* Genesis 7

CHAPTER EIGHT

1. *Midrash Rabbah, Ecclesiastes* 8:1
2. Talmud, *Avoda Zora,* p. 4a
3. *B'nai Yisroel,* Pekuday
4. *Ahavath Dodim,* Song of Songs 3:1
5. Talmud, *Berochoth,* p. 32b
6. Oral Tradition
7. Old Parables
8. Talmud, *Sabbath,* p. 30a
9. *Midrash Rabbah, Lamentation* 3
10. Rashi, Talmud, *Sanhedrin,* p. 44b
11. Talmud, *Gittin, p.* 56b
12. *Tshuvas Hagaonim,* Rav Hai Gaon 13
13. *Midrash Rabbah, Esther* 7
14. *Sefer Massioth, L'Rabbainu Nissim Gaon*
15. Talmud, *Berochoth,* p. 58a
16. Targum, *Tehillim* 57:1-3; *Midrash, Tehillim* 34; *Exempla of Rabbis,* p. 418, Gaster
17. *Mogen Avoth* 4:4, Shiman ben Zemach Duran

CHAPTER NINE

1. Talmud, *Berochoth,* p. 60b
2. *Beth Ha'bchirah* 3:19, Rabbi Menachem Ha'me'eri
3. *Machzor Vitry, Pirke Avoth* 3:20, Rabbainu Simcha

4. *Harvard Classics,* Vol. 17, p. 39
5. Talmud, *Sabbath,* p. 30a
6. Job 3:17,18,19
7. *Midrash Rabbah, Ecclesiastes* 9:7
8. *Midrash Rabbah, Ecclesiastes* 9:8
9. Talmud, *Yevomoth,* p. 62b; *Exempla of Rabbis,* p. 355, Gaster; *Midrash Rabbah, Song of Songs* 1
10. Talmud, *Kethuboth,* p. 67b
11. Talmud, *Horioth,* p. 10a
12. *Ethics of the Fathers* 3:20
13. *Ohel Yaacov,* Nasso
14. Talmud, *Tammid,* p. 32a
15. II Samuel 20:15-22
16. Talmud, *Berochoth,* p. 61a
17. *Midrash David* 1:1, Rabbainu David Hanagid
18. Talmud, *Kidushin,* p. 40a

CHAPTER TEN

1. *Kol Yaacov, Koheleth* 5:1
2. *Ohel Yaacov,* Vayigash
3. *Mishlay Shu'olim,* Brachia Hanakdan
4. *Derech Eretz Rabbah,* Chapter IV
5. Talmud, *Rosh Hashana,* p. 19a
6. Talmud, *Pesochim,* p. 50a
7. *Midrash Rabbah, Dvorim* I
8. Talmud, *Sukah,* p. 53a; *Ethics of the Fathers* 2:7; *Midrash Rabbah, Ecclesiastes* 10:8
9. Talmud, *Baba Kamma,* p. 50a
10. *Dubno Maggid,* Vol. II, p. 264, Israel J. Zevin
11. *Ohel Yaacov,* Kedoshim
12. Talmud, *Eruvin,* p. 54b
13. *Ohel Yaacov,* Mikaytz
14. *Mishlay Shu'olim,* Brachia Hanakdan
15. *Harvard Classics,* Vol. 17, p. 19
16. I Kings 12:17

17. I Kings 3:16-28
18. Talmud, *Kethuboth*, p. 59b
19. *Midrash Rabbah, Genesis* 33
20. Talmud, *Baba Bathra*, p. 3b

CHAPTER ELEVEN

1. *Midrash Rabbah, Ecclesiastes* 11:1
2. Talmud, *Taanith*, p. 24a
3. Talmud, *Sabbath*, p. 77b
4. Talmud, *Chagigah*, p. 3a
5. *Tifereth Yehudah,* Baal Shemtov
6. *Midrash Zuta, Ruth* 4:11
7. Talmud, *Sanhedrin*, p. 98b
8. Talmud, *Eruvin*, p. 54a
9. *Midrash Rabbah, Ecclesiastes* 11:9
10. Talmud, *Sabbath*, p. 30b

CHAPTER TWELVE

1. *Shivchai Tzadikim*, p. 32, M. Citrin
2. Talmud, *Baba Metzia*, p. 87a
3. Talmud, *Baba Metzia*, p. 87a
4. Talmud, *Sabbath*, p. 152a
5. *Midrash Rabbah, Ecclesiastes* 12:5
6. *Midrash Rabbah, Ecclesisastes* 5:10
7. Oral Tradition
8. *Tifereth Hatzadikim,* A. Kahn
9. *Midrash Rabbah, Song of Songs* 1:1
10. *Midrash Rabbah, Song of Songs* 1:1
11. Talmud, *Sabbath*, p. 31a
12. *Midrash Rabbah, Ecclesiastes* 12:12; Talmud, *Eruvin,*
    p. 21b; Talmud *Megillah*, p. 9a; *Yalkut Me'Ahm Lo-
    ayz,* p. 37, Rabbi Yaacov Kolay
13. Talmud, *Makkoth*, p. 23b
14. Talmud, *Yoma*, p. 35b

GLOSSARY

Aleph-Beth ——————————————— Hebrew Alphabet

Chassid (pl. Chassidim) ——————————— The Pious Ones

Gehinom ——————————————————— Hell

Halacha ———————— Law, legal decisions of the Rabbis

Havdala ————— (Separation) ritual marking the conclusion
of the Sabbath or a Holy Day

Koheleth ————————————————— Book of Ecclesiastes

Menorah ——————————— Seven branched candelabra

Midrash ——————————————— Homiletic literature

Mishna ————— Earliest part of oral law based on the Bible

Mitzva (pl. Mitzvot) ————— Commandment; a good deed

Talmud —— Books of oral law consisting of legal, ethical and
homiletic interpretation of the Bible

Tefilin ———————————————————— Phylacteries

Torah ———— Teaching; Five Books of Moses; often refers
to the entire religious literature

Yeshiva ————————————————— Talmudical College

Zohar ———————————— Books of Jewish mysticism

Zuz (pl. Zuzim) ——————————— Silver coin or coins

INDEX TO THE STORIES

CHAPTER THREE

CHAPTER FOUR

CHAPTER FIVE

CHAPTER EIGHT

CHAPTER ELEVEN

CHAPTER TWELVE